Tokyo Vegan Guide

The Plant-Based Foodie's Guide to Japan's Capital

Chiara Park Terzuolo

Foreword

While writing the 2017 edition of the Tokyo Vegan Guide I got the opportunity to chat with many vegan chefs, and it is clear that the plant-based trend is now here to stay. 2018 is proving to be a stellar year for vegan foodies in Tokyo, with dozens of wonderful new restaurants popping up across the city and interesting collaborations between non-vegan restaurants and plant-based chefs.

When I arrived in Japan's sprawling capital over 8 years ago, I was a vegetarian with high standards but almost no budget. Over the years I was able to start eating out more regularly and started transitioning towards veganism, and my search for restaurants and stores that could supply delicious and satisfying cruelty-free meals started to occupy a good deal of my time. In the last few years it has become increasingly easy to find excellent vegan cuisine, partially due to the fact that veganism is more prevalent in Japan than vegetarianism, which is due to a few major cultural factors.

The first is historical, going back to pre-Meiji era Japan when raising and selling animals for consumption was banned, due to the strong Buddhist edicts of the time. The traditional Japanese diet, before the changes made to 'modernize' the country during the Meiji era, was mainly based on barley, rice, miso, veggies, occasional fish and more rarely still meat (used for 'medicinal' purposes). We can still see echoes of this diet in *shojin ryori*, the cuisine of Buddhist monks, who in general also avoid eggs and pungent vegetables like garlic and onions.

As for milk products, these are still a relatively recent addition to the Japanese diet, introduced first during the Meiji era, when thinkers of the time believed that dairy and meat products would make the population stronger and more similar to the Europeans with whom they had started to trade and create political alliances. During the United States' occupation of Japan after World War II, the authorities pushed the use of milk products to boost protein consumption for children.

The other aspect that gives veganism a leg up is the high prevalence and trendiness of macrobiotic cuisine. Many cafés and restaurants in Japan, including some in this guide, label themselves as macrobiotic rather than vegan. While the basic principle behind it is quite different, a health regimen rather than an ethical choice, on the whole macrobiotic diets are very close to veganism.

Popularized by Georg Ohsawa and Michio Kushi, macrobiotic diets in Japan usually revolve around locally grown produce, cereals, miso, and beans, using little oil and mild seasonings. The occasional use of naturally-raised fish and meat products means that macrobiotic cuisine is not necessarily completely plant-based; however, shops and restaurants that run on these principles will be more aware of your needs as a vegan.

How to Use the Guide

Tokyo itself is the most frequently visited city in Japan and is endlessly fascinating even to those of us who live within its concrete embrace. While there are many areas which are pleasant for a stroll and harbor hidden vegan hot spots but do not offer sights of great note, I understand that most visitors to Tokyo have limited time in the city and the idea of traveling 40 to 60 minutes just for a meal would be difficult. For this reason I have tried to introduce as many restaurants as possible around areas which travelers are likely to visit.

To make it easier to navigate, the restaurants have been grouped by area according to the closest station/area of sights, and I have provided some background information about things to do and see nearby, so that you don't have to switch back and forth between guides to be able to know what cool stuff is near the cafés and restaurants.

Tokyo has a rap of being a very expensive city, and this is not completely true. However, things that are trendy or seen as 'alternative' or healthy tend to have a higher price tag attached. Be prepared to spend between 1000 to 1500 yen for a filling lunch, and closer to 2500 to 3000 yen for dinner. I have done my best to include options for all budgets and provided price guidelines for each restaurant. In the Helpful Hints section, you will find tips for navigating convenience stores, supermarkets and other cheaper, on-the-go options.

Criteria for Choosing the Restaurants

While in Japan veganism is often considered a stoic, health-based choice due to being confused with macrobiotic diets, there is no reason that vegan cuisine should be boring or flavorless. When going out to eat one doesn't want just another meal, but something that makes your eyes light up at the flavors dancing along your tongue. The eateries selected for this guide are those which provide (in my personal opinion) exactly that experience. My lifelong love of good food, excellent wine and proper presentation are not in one bit affected by my choice to live as cruelty-free an existence as possible. I greatly value a fully pleasurable dining experience.

I visited each restaurant at least twice, if possible at different times and days of the week, to check for consistency and quality. No meals were comped, and it was only after this guide was completed that the restaurant owners were informed that they were to be included, so all opinions are my own. On a few counts I have included restaurants that, while not to my personal taste, have been rated highly by fellow vegan gourmands.

When traveling, the experience of trying local dishes is one of the great pleasures of visiting a new country. Delicious as they may be, veggie burgers and burritos are not what one associates with Japan. Although many Western-style and Western-influenced joints have made the list, I have tried to give pride of place to restaurants which offer Japanese or locally-influenced cuisine, so that you can experience the flavors of Japan without having to compromise your beliefs.

Most of the cafés and restaurants included in this guide are 100% vegan, for peace of mind and to allow for the thrill of having the whole menu to choose from. For the macrobiotic and 'mixed' restaurants, only those which are very clear about veganism and which can be trusted to take your requests seriously have been included.

Besides vegans, I have tried to include many places which can cater to those with gluten free, vegetarian or even raw diets. All this information is included in each review, so you can check at a glance. As basically all vegan cuisine is also appropriate for those who keep halal—with the exception of dishes which contain alcohol—kosher or are Hindu, I hope that this guide will help as many people as possible have a wonderful, food-filled trip to Japan's capital.

You will also find a selection of 'Other Options' for some areas. The spots listed here are for restaurants and cafés that, while offering vegan food options, are not my top recommended spots for various reasons. But, since we are all different in matters of taste, I thought it would be good to give readers the option of checking them out!

Wait, What About...?

Those familiar with Tokyo or the excellent Happy Cow app may notice that not all of Tokyo's vegan restaurants are listed. No disrespect is meant to any of these establishments, in fact, a few of my personal favorites have not made the cut! My reasons for not including them are not necessarily due to the quality of the cuisine.

Selections were made taking into consideration location, opening hours, uniqueness of the dishes served and the likelihood of survival in Tokyo's famously competitive restaurant scene. After eight years in the city, my barometer for restaurant success is finely tuned, and I want to avoid visitors trekking to a joyfully anticipated restaurant only to be disappointed to find it has since closed, wasting precious time during a trip or weekend.

With that in mind, thank you for deciding to pick up this guide, and happy eating!

Popular Sightseeing Spots

As the biggest city in the world, Tokyo literally has something for everyone. From the traditional (Asakusa, Yanaka) to the modern (Roppongi, Tokyo Station) and subculture (Akihabara, Nakano) to natural beauty (Shinjuku Park, Ueno), there is always something new to explore!

For first-time visitors, the metro system may seem a bit overwhelming, but there are plenty of maps, apps and websites—not to mention the wonder of Google Maps—to help you figure out how to get to your next destination. The government and other service providers have also been putting a lot more effort into providing English, Chinese and Korean signage, and it is now common to find English-speaking staff in most large stations. To save money, make sure to take advantage of the various special train passes available to visitors, or at least get a Suica or Pasmo rechargeable train card to avoid constantly having to buy tickets.

If you are having trouble, don't hesitate to ask. Like in many big cities worldwide, most Tokyoites actually come from other areas of the country and so once had to figure out the ins-and-outs of the capital, so they can empathize with your struggle.

Shinjuku

Home to one of the city's largest and most confusing train and metro stations, Shinjuku is a central juncture and is where many of Tokyo's citizens come to shop in the numerous department stores, enjoy a night out or catch up with friends.

When arriving at Shinjuku Station by train, be sure to double-check exactly which exit you need to take to get to your destination. It can be quite a hike from one side of the station to the other if you get it wrong.

One of the highlights of this area is Shinjuku Gyoen, a large park which has some fine Japanese gardens, beautiful *sakura* (cherry blossoms) in spring, red autumn leaves and centennial trees that provide a spectacular contrast with the towering skyscrapers on the horizon. A bit racier (but still quite safe for visitors), the streets of Kabukicho are filled with neon signs and huge posters of hostesses, hosts and services that are probably best left untranslated. The popular Robot Restaurant, Samurai Museum and Godzilla statue are also found here.

Not far from the park is the warren of bars known as Golden Gai. Some of these small drinking spots are very visitor friendly, and the little alleys harken back to Shinjuku's humble beginnings as an area for travelers and day laborers. Pop by the nearby shrine, Hanazono Jinja, which is nicely spooky at night.

LGBTQ visitors will want to visit the Ni Chome area, home to Tokyo's largest concentration of gay/lesbian/queer spaces, with Arty Farty and Airi being two good spots to start your evening.

A quick zip through the unfortunately named Shomben Yokocho (Piss Alley) is sufficient, and if you want a good (and above all, free!) view of the city, head over to the Tokyo Metropolitan Government Building and ride the elevator all the way to the top.

Kiboko

Address: Shimura Bldg 4F, 2-5-8 Shinjuku, Shinjuku-ku, Tokyo
How to get there: right by the C5 exit of Shinjuku Sanchome Station. Look for the Doutor coffee shop, it is on the fourth floor of the same building (the windows are decorated with hippos).
Opening hours: Thursday through Saturday from 16:00 to 22:00, Sundays and holidays 15:00 to 21:00 (last order 20:00).
Price: starting from around 1000 yen for a drink and sweets during café hours, about 3000~5000 for dinner with a glass of wine.

Kiboko (which means hippopotamus in Swahili) has an enviable location right by Shinjuku Gyoen Park and the Shinjuku Sanchome metro station. Perched on the fourth floor above a large Doutor coffee shop, the owner/chef does a remarkable job of dishing out yummy wine bar food and *izakaya* (Japanese pub) style fare accompanied by bio wines. While the menu changes seasonally, there are a few standout items which are always available. The coriander-stuffed *gyoza* potstickers are completely addictive, and the trippa-style stew is complex and robust, with a pleasing kick of tomato. The eggless Spanish *tortilla* omelette is creamy and comforting, perfect after a long day of walking around. Make sure to leave space for the fruit tarts, which are imaginative and filled with nutty goodness.

Ain Soph Ripple

Address: Nissho Bldg 1F, Kabukicho 2-46-8, Shinjuku-ku, Tokyo
How to get there: from JR Shinjuku Station's East Exit hang left and follow the road. On you left you should see the Odakyu and Palette buildings in the distance. Keep

following the sidewalk (without crossing) until you pass them. Directly in front, you should see the Pepe building, which looks like a brown chimney stack. Cross the road while aiming for that building, and take the road that runs straight between Pepe and a pachinko parlor. Keep going straight until the Green Plaza Shinjuku capsule hotel, then take a right. Take the next left and walk almost all the way down, past Okubo Park. Look for the blue wave sign on your left.
Opening hours: Monday through Friday, 11:00 to 21:30 and Saturday, Sundays and holidays 11:00 to 20:30.
Price: budget around 1100~1600 yen for a set meal.

Ripple is the newest member of Tokyo's vegan Ain Soph restaurant group, and by far my favorite among them. More down to earth and budget friendly, this hidden spot in the Kabukicho area is an ideal place for a quick lunch or impromptu dinner. The menu is small and focuses on American and Tex-Mex influenced classics such as burgers, burritos and fries, as well as a few salads and (if you are lucky) their rich mac&cheese. English-speaking staff and menus are on hand, a nice break if you are a bit tired of deciphering Japanese menus. While the food is not Japanese at all, the friendliness of the staff and limited-time desserts are enough reason to stop by. If you keep halal, a few of their items are completely alcohol-free as well.

Chaya Macrobiotics Isetan

Address: Shinjuku Isetan Main Building 7F, 3-14-1 Shinjuku, Shinjuku-ku, Tokyo
How to get there: follow the signs in Shinjuku Sanchome Station directing you to the Isetan Department store (or find exits B3 or B4), and go up to the restaurant floor.
Opening hours: open daily (except on days the department store is closed) from 11:00 to 22:00.
Price: this is a relatively classy restaurant, located in an upscale department store. Expect 2000~4000 yen for lunch and 4000~7000 yen for dinner, depending on menu choices.

A nice spot for a bit of a splurge, Chaya is about as far away as you can get from the 'hippy' image of veganism. White table clothes, elegant wood decor and lovely presentation are some of the drawing points of this Tokyo institution. The cuisine is available in course sets, an interesting veggie-friendly introduction to Japanese concepts of old-school Western dishes such as croquettes, terrines and hamburger 'steaks' with demi-glace sauce. The Chaya Macrobi course is usually the best value as it also includes a drink and your choice of dessert. As macrobiotic diets are not necessarily vegan, do note that there will be some amount of fish on the menu, with vegan choices. The dessert menu, however, is entirely vegan, and is both beautiful and completely scrumptious. If you are on a budget opt for a slice of cake or patisserie and a cup of coffee as an afternoon treat. Visitors who are looking for gluten free or oriental vegetarian (no pungent vegetables) options will also be satisfied. For a less expensive option, look up their Hibiya branch, which you can read about in the Ginza section of this guide.

Other Options in the Shinjuku Area

Futaba Fruits Parlor

Address: Marui Main Bldg 5f, 3-30-13 Shinjuku, Shinjuku-ku, Tokyo
How to get there: located inside the Marui department store, which is directly connected to Shinjuku Sanchome Station via Exit A1, or is just a short walk from Exit A4.
Opening hours: Monday through Saturday from 11:00 to 21:00, and Sundays and holidays from 11:00 to 20:30 (last order 30 minutes before closing).
Price: around 930~1380 yen for a meal or a sundae, 630~980 yen for vegan cakes.

Surprisingly cozy despite being housed inside a department store, this café is a sister shop to Wired Bonbon (included in the Sweets and Treats section of this guide).

While they do have a few decent food options, such as the creamy avocado and vegetable gratin and tofu-based taco rice, the main draw here is the dessert menu. The incredible stacked ice cream parfaits can basically all be made vegan for an extra 100 yen, including the thick and satisfying whipped cream. Most of the fluffy fruit-topped pancakes are gluten free, or can be made so on request, and even their cream *anmitsu* (a dessert with agar jelly, fruit, red bean paste and black sugar syrup) can be veganized, in case you want to try a more traditional Japanese dessert. Vegan and gluten free options are marked, however most of the text is Japanese so ask the friendly staff for a bit of help if you get confused.

Ain Soph Journey

Address: Shinjuku Q Bldg, 3-8-9 Shinjuku, Shinjuku-ku, Tokyo
How to get there: right outside the C5 Exit of Shinjuku Sanchome Station.
Opening hours: open daily. Weekdays lunch is from 11:00 to 17:00 (last order 16:00) and dinner from 18:00 to 22:00 (last order 22:00). On weekends from 11:00 to 23:00 (last order 22:00).
Price: from 1800 yen for lunch, and budget at least 3000 to 4000 yen for dinner.

While it is almost blasphemous to mention to Tokyo vegans that you are not a fan of this very famous spot, Ain Soph seems a bit expensive for their offerings of simple, Western-style vegan food. The curries are nicely comforting, but the portions for the lunch courses are quite small. If you are looking for a brunch spot, the fluffy pancakes (which also are available in seasonal versions) and the hot chai cocktail are top-notch.

Shibuya

Tourists flock to the famous Scramble Crossing and the younger crowd goes to Shibuya to party, usually meeting up in front of Hachiko, the famous statue of the dog who waited for her beloved but sadly departed owner in front of the station. During Halloween, this is the place to be seen, with the entire area shut off to traffic to allow for costumed revels.

Shibuya has a plethora of shopping options including the rather awesome Loft store, and a few smaller gems like Nombei Yokocho (a little street of bars, similar to Golden Gai in Shinjuku) and Dogenzaka, also known as Love Hotel Hill, where you can still see a few of the more over-the-top facades. Quite close to both Harajuku and Daikanyama, taking a stroll to your next destination around the smaller streets is a good opportunity to discover unusual fashion and even odder specialty stores. Art lovers should stop by the overhead pass of the Shibuya Mark City shopping/station building, where you can see the Japanese artist Taro Okamoto's huge mural, "The Myth of Tomorrow". This is also a good photo spot to get a view of the Scramble Crossing without getting crushed. Music buffs will love Tower Records, the country's largest music store.

Yaffa Organic Cafe

Address: 3-27-5 Shibuya, Shibuya-ku, Tokyo
How to get there: from the New South Exit of JR Shibuya Station take a right. Cross the street and take the first side street on the left. The restaurant is on the ground floor of the Tokyu Stay hotel's annex.
Opening hours: open daily, lunch is from 11:30 to 15:00 and dinner from 18:00 to 22:00.
Price: 1100~1500 yen for lunch (a little more on weekends), around 3000~4000 yen for dinner.

Although the location has changed from time to time, this restaurant has been gracing Tokyo with its presence since 2000. While like many organic restaurants in Japan it does serve meat and fish, the menu is heavily centered around the fresh veggies sent in weekly from organic farms around the country. The staff is knowledgeable about veganism, and the menu clearly marks which dishes are free of animal products. Lunch is pretty basic, with a choice of sets involving salad, pasta, brown rice and soup, which change daily. In the evening the menu evolves into something more European-inspired, as the chef turns out well-balanced gratinees, creamy pasta with *ooba*-laced pesto and other tidbits like deep-fried avocado or prettily presented bean-filled salads. The vegan-friendly dessert menu is sadly limited to simple dried-fruit-filled 'Irish scones', but the wine menu and unusual hot drinks help fill this gap.

Nagi Shokudo

Address: Royal Palace Shibuya 103, 15-10 Uguisudanicho, Shibuya-ku, Tokyo
How to get there: from the JR South Exit of Shibuya Station take a left and climb the stairs to the pedestrian overpass. Go straight across and go down the stairs, keep walking to the left (passing the large guitar store) and then take a right. Go straight up the hill and keep going until you see the Shibuyasakuragaoka Post Office on your left. Right across the road in the basement of the building in front of you (under an Italian restaurant) you will find Nagi Shokudo. Look for the small red sign.
Opening Hours: open Monday through Saturday, lunch 12:00 to 16:00 (last order 15:00), dinner 18:00 to 23:00. Open for lunch on Sunday.
Price: 1000~1500 yen for lunch sets, budget around 2500~3000 for dinner and a drink.

The oldest vegan restaurant in Shibuya, Nagi Shokudo has been serving local and visiting vegans, as well as people working nearby, for almost 10 years. Often reviewed very highly both online and in guidebooks, during my three visits the dishes seem to have been a bit hit or miss. The menu is built around three main set plates; a set with fried soy meat with a sauce, a curry set and a set where you can choose 3 daily deli options. Portions are definitely Japanese-sized. The fried soy meat, which I tried both in a chili sauce and a Chinese chive sauce, is reliably good, and the miso soup is subtle and not overly salty. The daily deli selections range from excellent (a chilled pasta salad with fresh spinach) to disappointing (*enoki* mushrooms and celery in an indefinable sauce), but this may be a seasonal issue. The curries are reliable, if not powerfully spiced. The interior is faded but not unwelcoming. Tall diners will struggle with the low chairs and tables. A better value at lunch rather than dinner- check it out if you are in Shibuya or Daikanyama and decide how you feel about it for yourself.

Tokyo Station Area

Tokyo Station is the main hub for *shinkansen* (bullet trains) and a grand intersection for various, not quite as speedy train lines from all ends of the city. This huge station is also quite close to the Imperial Palace, Nihonbashi and Ginza areas. The original section of the station, which dates back to the early 1900s, is a lovely piece of Meiji architecture worth a look, particularly at night when it is fully lit up.

Nearby you will find the Imperial Palace, surrounded by a moat and a constant loop of runners, as well as the large Imperial East Gardens. Home to many of Tokyo's first Western-style buildings and offices, it is not unusual to see lovely red brick structures peeking out among the towering skyscrapers. If so inclined you can enter a few of these buildings such as the Mitsubishi Ichigokan Museum, which specializes in Western art. The attached Café 1894 is not vegan but nonetheless a lovely spot for a cup of tea surrounded by elegant wooden columns and highly polished brass.

Within the station, it is easy to get lost amongst the hundreds of shops, restaurants, entrances and suited "salarymen" rushing to and fro. However, it is worth braving the labyrinth, as Tokyo Station is home to two of the city's best vegan ramen joints!

T's TanTan

Address: Keiyo Street in JR Tokyo Station, 1-9-1 Marunouchi, Chiyoda-ku, Tokyo
How to get there: the shop is located inside the station gates, so you will need to buy a ticket if you are not already inside. It is in the 'Keiyo Street' near the entrance to the Keiyo line, which is not too far from the gates for the bullet train. Follow the signs for the red Keiyo line.
Opening hours: open daily from 07:00 to 23:00 (last order at 22:30).
Price: 800~1000 yen for a bowl of ramen, side dishes between 200~450 yen.

One of the first, and best, vegan ramen joints in town. Their specialty is obviously *tantan* (ground meat) ramen, of which they offer 5 different varieties, all fragrant with sesame oil and with enough oomph to win over carnivores. The black sesame ramen and faux-*tonkotsu* pork marrow broth are also powerful, the perfect thing to dig into on a chilly day. Make sure you go hungry, as you will want to try their irresistible *karaage* fried 'chicken' or even go for the mini Japanese-style curry rice. Be prepared for a bit of a line during peak times, but the staff move guests along swiftly. In any case, if you are like me, you will need the time to ponder the menu and second-guess yourself repeatedly.

Sora no Iro NIPPON

Address: Ramen Street in First Avenue Tokyo Station, 1-9-1 Marunouchi, Chiyoda-ku, Tokyo
How to get there: the shop is located in the Ramen Street in the basement floor of Tokyo Station's First Avenue shopping area, which is most easily accessible from the Yaesu Exit side of the station, near the Daimaru department store. The shops can be a bit hard to find, check the maps on the walls of First Avenue for directions to the Ramen Street.
Opening hours: daily from 08:30 to 23:00 (last order at 22:30).

Price: between 1000~1200 yen per bowl, depending on toppings.

Earning a mention in the Michelin Guide, Sora no Iro's version of ramen is both inventive and colorful. Instead of recreating flavors common to meat-based soups, they draw out the full depth of flavor from vegetables, creating a hearty creamy base for the noodles, which are then garnished with seasonal veggies. The noodles, which are thinner in order to balance out the rich soup, are spiked with red bell pepper. A satisfying gluten free version made from brown rice is also available. The interior is surprisingly whimsical, and Miyazaki fans will be delighted to see several nods to the director's beloved Ghibli animations. A recommendation is to go after 16:00 when they serve a limited number of *tantan* bowls. Beware of the side salad, as the dressing is not vegan, but feel free to round off your meal with a cup of their soft-serve ice cream or a green smoothie.

Ginza

Strolling through Ginza is an opportunity to walk all over some of Japan's most expensive real estate, with certain spots going for 27 million yen per square meter!

As such, it is not surprising that the broad walkways glitter with designer shops, busy department stores and lots of famous restaurants and bars. One of the best times to see the area is right at sunset, as the signs flicker on and you can get a feeling for what this chic part of town must have been like during the "Bubble Era" in the late 80's. The side streets are equally interesting, with many high-class hostess bars and members-only clubs, with some buildings filled with them from top to toe.

Be sure to stop by the renovated Kabukiza theater, for which you can often get cheap 'one scene' tickets on performance days, to get a taste for this dramatic art where performances often last several hours. Stationary fans will love both Itoya and Kyukyodo, where wonderful paper, writing utensils and notebooks await. The Ginza

5 mall has many tiny shops, including a few antiques and kimono stores worth a browse, and the brand new Ginza 6 is making waves.

For a matcha tea experience with a difference, Chanoha in the basement of the Matsuya department store is one of the most serene spots in the city. If you don't want to wait, they have excellent take out options (the green tea mixed with soda water being particularly good on a hot day). Right next door is a tiny sake bar, perfect for tasting a few cups of the county's famous rice wine.

Although not vegan, beneath the tracks between Ginza and TokyoStation you can see hundreds of small pubs and restaurants, a slip back in time to an older, less-polished Tokyo.

Chaya Natural & Wild Table

Address: Toho Hibiya Bldg B2F, 1-2-2 Yurakucho, Chiyoda-ku, Tokyo
How to get there: a bit of a walk from Ginza's main street, the restaurant is closer to Hibiya Station. From Exit A4 of Hibiya Station turn immediately to the right, facing away from the green overhead train tracks. Walk straight and take a left right before the crosswalk. Go straight past the small Godzilla statue. You should see the large 'Chanter' sign on a building straight ahead. The restaurant is in the B2 floor of this building.
Opening hours: Tuesday through Saturday 11:00 to 23:00 (last order at 22:30) and Monday and Sunday 11:00 to 22:00 (last order at 21:30).
Price: 1300~2000 yen for lunch, 2000~4000 yen for dinner. Cakes for around 600 yen, and cake sets for 980 yen.

A more casual branch of the macrobiotic Chaya group, this spot is hidden away in the basement of the Chanter department store. The food is served with practiced reliability, and this particular spot tends to have less fish/meat than other branches.

The fact that they serve food all day, as well as their famous vegan cakes, make this a reliable stand-by when checking out the Ginza/Hibiya area. The simple but homey cuisine is *yoshoku* (Japanese versions of Western standards), with soy milk-based stews, satisfying saucy hamburger steaks and fresh deli plates that get swapped out seasonally. The desserts are worth an extra splurge, and you can add one to your lunch for 200 yen. As Japan's most popular cake, the strawberry shortcake is a must-try and is not overly sweet with nice juicy berries taking pride of place. During dinner a few additional entrees and set courses are available, with creative pasta and nicely presented appetizers giving extra flair. The location can feel a bit sterile, so for a more elegant meal check out the Isetan branch, reviewed in the Shinjuku section of this guide. One or two gluten free dishes and desserts are always available.

Kyushu Jangara Ramen

Address: 6-12-17, Ginza, Chuo-ku, Tokyo
How to get there: go straight out of Ginza Station's Exit A4, then turn left at the first intersection. Keep going straight until you pass the Ginza Six building on your right. Cross the street and take another right, you should see the shop's bright blue, rainbow-decorated sign just ahead.
Opening hours: open daily from 10:45, closes at 23:00 except on Friday when they close at 03:00
Price: 1000 yen for the vegan ramen, about 90~200 yen for various vegan toppings

Although more down to earth than many of the fancy eateries in Ginza, Kyushu Jangara's bright *noren* curtain and eclectic decor make for a truly cheerful ramen experience. While mostly famous for their non-vegan *tonkotsu* ramen, this small chain offers one truly satisfying vegan bowl. Firm noodles float in a *umami*-rich soy sauce-based soup, to which you can add an additional kick by sprinkling in condiments like hot pepper or milled garlic. Toppings are simple, but the star of the show is their meat-free *chashu*. Usually made from braised pork, Jangara's version is created using layered tofu skin, called *yuba*, soaked in a delightfully savory-sweet sauce then lightly charred.

Besides Ginza, they also have branches in Harajuku, Akihabara, Nihonbashi and Ikebukuro.

Harajuku/Omotesando

One of Tokyo's major fashion spots, visitors can spot women in lolita dress passing by gleaming, designer storefronts, and huge lines patiently waiting in front of the popular sweets shops *du jour*. This focus on fashion means that vegan-friendly joints are plentiful. After window shopping on Omotesando, considered the Champs Elysees of Tokyo, and braving the brightly-dressed teenagers on Takeshita Street, make sure to stroll through the Meiji Shrine for a breath of fresh air and the chance to catch a peek of a traditional Shinto wedding procession. The little Ota Museum is a charming spot, with an excellent collection of *ukiyoe* prints. Although a bit of a trek, the nearby Nezu Museum is also a must-see, with a fantastic Japanese-style garden and very photogenic tea houses. Give yourself time to wander the back streets of Omotesando, which tend to be quieter, yet offer a plethora of interesting discoveries. The Omotesando/Aoyama area has a particularly high number of vegan restaurants and cafés, so choosing a hotel nearby or with an easy train connection may be a good idea to ensure you can check out as many as possible.

8ablish

Address: **5-10-17-2F, Minami Aoyama, Minato-ku, Tokyo**
How to get there: from the B1 Exit of Omotesando Station, walk straight and cross the large street right in front of you. Keep going straight, and turn immediately into the first little street on your left (if you pass Aoyama University you have gone too far). You will find the staircase up to the entrance on your left.

Opening hours: Monday to Friday lunch from 11:30 to 14:30 and dinner from 18:00 to 22:00. Saturdays and Sundays from 11:30 to 22:00 (last order 30 minutes before closing).

Price: 1200~1500 yen for lunch, budget 3000~4500 yen for dinner without wine.

Few vegan restaurants in Tokyo stand up to repeated visits as well as 8ablish, part of the same company as the much-beloved Pure Café, which sadly closed in 2016. The inventive daily specials, well-balanced seasonings and complete 180° departure from common Japanese-vegan menus make it one of the city's gems. The souvlaki (a Greek kebab dish) is reinvented using tempeh, nicely seared with spices and herbs. The daily specials run the gamut from British pub grub (a bubbling, creamy shepherd's pie with mushrooms) to a Japanese/Portuguese 'mix fried plate' of fried 'fish' with a punchy fresh tartar sauce, and everything in between. The dinner menu is expansive and beautifully presented, with prices to match. One of the standouts on a recent visit was the tofu ricotta ravioli in a caper-laced sauce, taking the usual vegan failsafe of pasta to another level.

Hanada Rosso

Address: Miyazaki Bldg 101, 6-28-5 Jingumae, Shibuya-ku, Tokyo

How to get there: the easiest way to get there is from Exit 7 of Meiji Jingumae Station. Turn right, and walk until a smaller back street joins the main road you are on. Look for the white tiled building, and go into the courtyard.

Opening hours: Weekdays lunch is from 11:30 to 16:00 (last order at 15:30) and dinner is from 17:30 to 21:00 (last order at 20:00). On weekends and holidays they are open from 12:00 to 21:00 (last order at 20:00).

Price: weekday lunches start at 1000 yen, weekends from 1,380 yen. A simple dinner will be around 2000~2500 yen per person. Desserts around 680 yen.

The *piece de resistance* here is without a doubt the demi-glace sauce covered 'hamburger steak', which skips any attempt of pretending it came from a cow and becomes an entirely different dish altogether. Fluffy- but not crumbly, moist- but not soggy, it pairs nicely with their staple brown rice and the daily veggie side dishes. The weekday lunch special is a great deal, and if you are looking for a more Japanese experience the sesame/miso cutlet's thick, *hatcho*-style miso provides a kick of umami. Good options for visitors with gluten allergies, as both the hamburger and curry are safe, however be forewarned that they have recently added some non-vegan selections to their menu.

Brown Rice Canteen

Address: 5-1-8 Jingumae, Shibuya-ku, Tokyo
How to get there: go straight out of Exit A1 of Omotesando Station, then take the first left. It is the fifth building on your right.
Opening Hours: daily from 11:30 to 18:00 (last order at 17:00).
Price: between 1500~1700 yen for lunch, with an extra 500 yen charge on weekends and holidays.

Run by the Neal's Yard cosmetics company, it is no surprise that the lunches here focus on simple, healthy ingredients presented in a beautiful, minimalist style. The daily lunch sets revolve around a main dish, often a tofu-based creation seasoned with miso, accompanied by rice, miso soup and two vegetable dishes (a traditional meal combination known as *ichiju sansai,* one soup and three sides). The steamed vegetable set is soothing, and the bean-based curry is quite mild with a nice balance of spices. The focus here is very Japanese in that the flavors of the vegetables are not tampered with, so don't expect fireworks. However it leaves one feeling so virtuous that you'll keep coming back. If you wish to dispel a bit of that aura of virtue, opt for one of the rich, seasonal desserts, but do make sure to check with the staff, as occasionally they use honey.

Tamana Shokudo

Address: 3-8-27 Minami Aoyama, Minato-ku, Tokyo
How to get there: from Exit A4 of Omotesando Station go right, and then take another right when you reach the large road called Aoyama Dori. Keep walking straight, passing the COMMUNE market on your right. After passing the market continue straight, and turn into the fourth side street on your right. It is a narrow street by a parking lot, and there should be a wooden sign with たまな食堂 written on it. Walk down the street and take the first left, the restaurant is just before the end of the cul de sac.
Opening hours: open daily, lunch available from 11:00 to 15:30 (last order 14:30), dinner from 18:00 to 22:30 (last order 21:30).
Price: 1350~1890 yen for lunch, vegan dinner courses between 2700~4000 yen, with a la carte options available.

Tamana has maintained its popularity since opening in 2011 despite the eccentric location thanks to the chef's signature dishes, which combine Japanese macrobiotic and fermented foods with tenants of Italian and French cuisine. The lunch sets all include a portion of their very fresh, colorful salads with handmade veggie-based dressings. Hungry visitors should opt for the *teishoku* (set meal) which changes daily and has a little bit of everything, including a small bowl of *natto* fermented soybeans, which are a bit of an acquired taste. The main dish for both the *teishoku* and rice bowl revolves around vegan variations of Japanese home cooking, such as a toothsome soy meat *shogayaki* (a gingery stir fry) or sweet and sour 'pork' *suubuta* with a nice kick of vinegar. The daily pasta dish is usually gluten free, but double check with the staff to make sure. On weekends getting there before noon is a good idea, as by 12:30 they are habitually packed. While the course dinners and a la carte selections are presented with practiced flourish, one should be aware that fish dishes do feature more prominently in the evening, which is a common practice in macrobiotic cooking.

Other Options in the Harajuku/Omotesando Area

Sincere Garden

Address: Aoyama Takano Bldg 2F, 3-5-4 Kitaaoyama, Minato-ku, Tokyo
How to get there: from Exit A3 of Omotesando Station walk straight and turn left immediately onto Aoyama Dori street (right by the Sanyodo bookstore). Walk straight for a few minutes, and the Sincere Spa will be on your left, a bit before the pedestrian bridge. The café is on the second floor. It is quite close to Tamana Shokudo.
Opening hours: daily from 11:30 to 20:00 (last order at 19:00), closed during New Years.
Prices: 1200~1600 yen for a meal, 400~700 yen for desserts. Take-out available.

Housed on the second floor of a small spa, the colorful dishes of this little café feature lots of salads, bright curries and a revolving selection of seasonal sweets. The portions may be a bit small for those with large appetites, but you can fill out your meal with one of their moist muffins or fresh bagels, often available in unusual flavors. Check out their seasonal specials, as you may be able to try vegan versions of Japanese favorites such as *chirashi zushi*, a 'scattered' sushi dish often served during the spring. English menus and a selection of gluten free options are available.

Mominoki House

Address: 2-18-5 Jingumae, Shibuya-ku, Tokyo
How to get there: from JR Harajuku Station's Takeshita Exit, cross the street and enter Takeshita Street. Keep on going straight until you reach the end of the street

and find yourself at the crosswalk of the large Meiji Dori street. Cross and take an immediate left onto the little Harajuku Street (look for the half-arch signs). Go straight down until you reach the end of the street, Take a right, cross the road and continue in the same direction. You should pass Streamers coffee on your right and a little after that there will be a yellow building. Right before the building take a left to find the restaurant.

Opening hours: lunch available daily from 11:00 to 15:00 (last order 14:30). Dinner between 17:00 and 22:00 (last order 21:00) from Monday to Saturday, and between 17:00 to 21:00 (last order 20:00) on Sunday.

Price: between 1000~1600 yen for lunch, budget around 4000 yen for dinner.

Chef Yamada has been offering healthy, pesticide-free veggie and brown rice-based meals since 1976, making this restaurant one of the longest-running macrobiotic restaurants in Tokyo. While there are a small number of meat or fish dishes on the menu, it is clear that the majority of diners come looking for vegan lunch sets and seasonal specials. The staples of Japanese macrobiotic cuisine are all present, with subtle seasoning and nicely chewy rice. The regular menu offers crunchy vegan cutlets and thick tofu steaks, but make sure to check out if there are any interesting seasonal dishes, such as noodles or lasagna. English-language menus and English-speaking staff are always on hand and there are a few gluten free options as well. While a bit pricey, the slightly hippy wooden decor and ease of ordering make this a safe bet for visiting vegans.

Natural House Aoyama Branch

Address: 3-6-18 Kitaaoyama, Minato-ku, Tokyo
How to get there: just across the street from Omotesando Station's B3 Exit. Look for the red apple logo.
Opening hours: daily from 10:00 to 22:00.
Price: anywhere between 500~1500 yen per person, depending on what you buy.

This organic/macrobiotic/health food supermarket is the largest of the Natural House chain which can be found in several locations around the city and in a few other spots across Japan. Natural House is an ideal spot to pick up a picnic lunch to enjoy in nearby Yoyogi Park. They offer a small selection of deli options, allowing you to mix and match, and also have a shared table in the back where you can sit and enjoy your meal if the weather is uncooperative. This is *the* place to try the vegan version of the Japanese *katsu sando* (cutlet sandwich), a beloved lunch time staple. The combination of the crisp cutlet, tangy sauce and layer of cabbage is strangely addictive. Keep an eye out for the cutlet-topped curry, called *katsu kare* in Japanese, another favorite cheap and cheerful businessperson's lunch. You can stock up on snacks (including gluten free and raw options) to keep on hand in case you need a quick pick-me up while sightseeing. Note that they often confusingly label foods as 'vegetarian' when they are actually vegan, so ask the staff if you want to double check.

Trueberry

Address: 3-10-25 Kitaaoyama, Minato-ku, Tokyo
How to get there: very close to Exit B2 of Omotesando Station
Opening hours: 10:00 to 19:00
Price: 800 yen and up for drinks, at least 1000 yen for a light meal
Check the information for the Hiroo shop for more details about the menu.

Asakusa Area

Always top on the list of places to visit in Tokyo, this traditional neighborhood is centered around hulking, red Sensoji Temple. From this point dozens of shopping streets radiate, the major one being Nakamisedori street which leads you straight to the temple from the Kaminarimon Gate, with its distinctive huge red lantern. While this can seem a touristy spot, the smaller covered shopping arcades and back streets of the area are more traditional, a jumble of tea houses, restaurants, interesting little shops and private homes. As you explore, keep your eyes peeled for the 'dangling houses' which are the symbol of the Hanayashiki, Japan's oldest amusement park. Entrance is only 1000 yen, and most of the quaintly retro rides are between 200 and 500 yen for one go, a bargain when compared to some of the country's larger theme parks!

Nearby you will also find Kappabashi, the kitchenware district, a great spot to find cute ceramics, plastic food samples and other oddities to bring home. Stretch your explorations out to the Kuramae district, which has a wonderful stationery shop, small-batch chocolate shop and a much more local feel. If you want, you can stroll all the way to Ueno on the *'butsudan'* road', a large road lined with Buddhist altar showrooms.

Dominating the horizon you will see the towering Tokyo Skytree, which at 634 meters is the tallest tower in the world and the second largest building in the world. You can ride up to decks at 350 or 450 meters, for views of the entire city. On clear days you can even see straight out to Mt. Fuji. The Solamachi complex at its feet has a huge selection of interesting gifts and goodies, and best of all, free wifi!

Kaemon Asakusa

Address: Visioncenter Asakusa 3F, Hanakawado 1-9-1, Taito-ku,Tokyo
How to get there: a short walk from Sensoji Temple. Find the Ekimise building (which is right above Tobu Asakusa Station) and locate the Tobu North exit. Facing away from the exit, turn to the left and walk until the streets branch out in several directions. Look for the Mini Stop convenience store, which is on the first floor of the building the restaurant is located inside.
Opening hours: closed on Tuesdays and Wednesdays, lunch from 11:00 to 14:30.
Price: buffet from 1200~1800 yen.

Vegan, organic and certified halal, oh my! One of Asakusa's few vegan joints, this odd little restaurant only operates a lunch buffet, which also includes tempting soups, salads and a tea bar. Skip the pasta, and take your pick of fried soy meat, tofu cutlets, veggie stews and curries. The food is pretty standard, but the large portions are a bonus after hours exploring the temple and nearby shopping streets. Don't mind the decor, as it does give the slight impression of being housed in an office. There is a prayer space for Muslim visitors, a considerate touch.

Sasaya Cafe

Address: 1-1-2 Yokokawa, Sumida-ku, Tokyo
How to get there: the restaurant is a 10 minute walk from the Tokyo Sky Tree. From Exit A1 of Tokyo Skytree Station (or from the plaza in front of the entrance to Sky Tree), turn left and cross the bridge over the small river. Cross the street at the intersection, and try to stay towards the right side of the road going straight ahead. Around half way you will pass the Salt and Tobacco Museum (on your right). At the large intersection with Kasuga Dori road you will cross again. Ahead of you and a bit to the right you should see some bamboo and the Sasaya Cafe sign, which has an image of Mt. Fuji.
Opening hours: daily (with occasional days off) from 08:30 to 18:00.
Price: between 700~1200 yen for a meal, around 500 yen for baked goods.

Housed in a renovated factory overlooking a section of the long, skinny Oyokogawa Koen park which runs between the Sky Tree and Kinshicho Station, Sasaya is surprisingly large and airy, a welcome addition in a city where niche restaurants tend towards the cramped. The menu is small, but happily also written in English. There is usually at least one gluten free option available which is less obvious, but the staff are happy to help. The Indian-style meals are comforting if not terribly potent, but the real standout is the fried tempeh cutlet, nicely crunchy on the outside and thick with fat soybeans. They have a rotating selection of sandwiches and monthly Asian inspired specials. If you are there bright and early, you may be rewarded by the appearance of tofu cheese toast, vegan quiche or freshly baked muffins, all of which pair nicely with the sweet, spicy masala chai.

Fucha Bon

Address: 1-2-11 Ryusen, Taito-ku, Tokyo
How to get there: although it is possible to walk there from Asakusa, it is quite a hike. Taking a taxi or walking from Iriya Station is much easier. From Iriya Station take Exit 3, and go straight ahead until you reach a crosswalk. Cross and take an immediate right. Continue on straight until you are almost at the end of the street. Take the last side street to the left (look for the white sign with the character 梵 on it) before reaching the wide road ahead. The restaurant is located in the second building on your left.
Opening hours: weekdays lunch is from 12:00 to 15:00 (last order 13:00) and dinner is from 17:00 to 21:00 (last order at 19:00). Saturday 12:00 to 21:00 (last order 19:00) and Sunday 12:00 to 20:00 (last order 18:00). Closed on Wednesday, New Year's holidays and some summer holidays. Making reservations by phone is highly recommended (03-3872-0375, basic English spoken).
Price: weekday lunch around 3450 or 5000 yen, courses available for 6000, 7000, 8000 or 10000 yen. Tax is not included.

The private *tatami* rooms, serene decor and refreshingly unpretentious, friendly service at Bon blow you away even before you have a chance to taste their *fucha* cuisine, a Chinese version of Japanese *shojin ryori* Buddhist meals. The restaurant has been around since 1972, originally aimed at serving Zen-influenced dishes at temple functions, and it is clear that it is still a popular spot for families to come together after attending various Buddhist rites. The procession of delicate, intricate dishes begins with a light tea and *rakugan* pressed-sugar sweet, and then takes off into a folly of seasonal tastes, with a fried *asagao* flower and faux abalone with lemon being just two highlights from a recent visit. A few staples of fucha are present in every meal, such as *unpen*, a ginger-laced, thickened soup made with leftover veggies which goes along with the waste-not philosophy of this cuisine. Other showstoppers are the intense sesame tofu and their famous fried eggplant covered in a hearty miso sauce. Light eaters and those on a budget should opt for the weekday lunch courses, as the more expensive courses are extremely filling. Make sure to wear matching, clean, hole-free socks, as you will be expected to remove your shoes before entering the *tatami* room.

Ueno

Home to one of the city's largest parks, bustling Ameyokocho shopping street and a high concentration of museums, you could easily spend a full day exploring this popular neighborhood.

Ueno Park is famous for being party-central during cherry blossom season, but has plenty to capture your interest in any season. Besides wandering under the leafy trees, the grounds house a seemingly unending number of spots to discover. Be sure to pass by Shinobazu Pond and stroll over to Bentendo Temple, located on a little island in the middle, which is particularly pretty in the summer when the lotus flowers are in bloom. The whole park is dotted with pretty temples, shrines, statues and even some seasonal flower gardens, as well as plenty of spots to stop for a cup of coffee or tea.

On rainy days the Tokyo National Museum, National Museum of Nature and Science, Tokyo Metropolitan Art Museum and surprisingly beautiful International Library of Children's Literature will keep you entertained for hours. However avoid the nearby zoo, as it likely to upset anyone who cares about animal welfare.

T's TanTan Ecute Ueno

Address: Ecute Ueno 3F, 7-1-1 Ueno, Taito-ku, Tokyo
How to get there: the shop is located inside the station gates, so you will need to buy a ticket if you are not already inside. The restaurant is easiest to reach from the Park or Iriya gates, and is across from Platform 8. Look for maps of the Ecute restaurant locations inside the station.
Opening hours: Monday to Saturday from 07:00 to 23:00, Sundays and holidays from 07:00 to 22:30 (last order 30 minutes before closing).
Price: 850~1500 yen for a meal, side dishes 250 yen.

The newest branch of the beloved T's Tantan vegan ramen shop in Tokyo Station, this shop offers three of their signature *tantan* ramen bowls, along with a small selection of Japanese soul food. The creamy 'cod roe' udon is a rare opportunity to try a vegan version of Japanese-style pasta dishes, while their ginger veggie-pork saute' set meal is perfect if you are famished. Side dishes like potato salad or T's justly famous *gyoza* dumplings only cost a couple hundred yen more, making this a great spot for a filling meal that is easy on the wallet. Top it all off with a cute panda ice cream, or get a couple *katsu* cutlet sandwiches to go, perhaps for a picnic in nearby Ueno Park.

Roppongi

One of Tokyo's party areas, particularly for the expat community, the main draw during the day are the many art galleries, such as the Mori Art Museum, located at the very top of vertiginous Mori Tower, as well as the Suntory Museum of Art and National Art Center. Visitors can also enjoy shopping opportunities and pleasant gardens near Tokyo Midtown. The Aoyama Cemetery is a nice spot for a quiet stroll, and a must-see during the cherry blossom season, when the tombs are lightened by fluffy *sakura* blossoms. Around November to Christmas, the Keyakizaka hill hosts wonderful winter illuminations.

Veganic to Go

Address: Nogizaka Studio 1F, 7-4-14 Roppongi, Minato-ku, Tokyo
How to get there: very close to Tokyo Midtown, from in front of the building (or near Exit 7 of Roppongi Station) walk towards the Mercedes Benz building, and turn left into the little street after the gas station.
Opening hours: Monday through Thursday, Sunday and national holidays from 11:30 to 17:00, Fridays and Saturdays from 11:30 to 22:00.
Price: 980 yen per burger, a bit more with extras

Don't be misled by the name, this little shop does have seating available, although it can be a bit close quarters at busy times. The menu is relatively small, and offers a selection of vegan/macrobiotic burgers, pizza and other sides, along with a few gluten free options and possibly the best vegan soft serve ice cream in town in seasonal flavors! Hands down, the thing to order on a first visit is the 'fish' burger, which is quite voluminous and drenched in glorious tartar sauce. For something a bit more local, the teriyaki burger is sumptuously glazed and satisfyingly messy. The buns contain both hemp and carbon, so you can feel vaguely self-satisfied about scarfing down this top-class vegan junk food. The desserts change seasonally, and are always a good bet, especially if the chocolate cake or ice cream is available. If you are on a budget, go on a Monday, as they have special deals for Meatless Monday.

Chien Fu

Address: SAI Bldg 4F, 3-1-22 Nishiazabu, Minato-ku, Tokyo
How to get there: from Roppongi Station Exit 1A, walk towards and then past Roppongi Hills (on your left). Cross the street, and walk on. Keep an eye out for the

Seven Eleven convenience store, you will find the entrance is right nearby it. It can be a bit tricky to find, as the restaurant is on the fourth floor.
Opening hours: daily from 11:00 to 21:30.
Price: between 1100~1500 yen for lunch, budget at least 3000 for dinner.

Perhaps one of the stranger vegan-friendly restaurants in Tokyo, Chien Fu dishes out Japanified Taiwanese food surrounded by faded faux-French tea room decor, with a view of the expressway. Nonetheless, the Taiwanese prowess at faux-meats is front and center here. The *mabo dofu* (spicy chili tofu), 'chicken' with cashew nuts and sweet and sour 'pork' are all excellent. You can even try out odd things like vegan squid and fish! The menu is clearly marked, indicating which options are vegan and which are vegetarian, and the elderly gentleman who seems to run the place is eager to help. Do keep in mind that Taiwanese cuisine tends to have less kick than mainland Chinese cooking, so choosing dishes with a bit of spice is probably your best option. Also, this is a good lunch spot, but may be a bit too quiet for dinner.

Other Options in Roppongi

AFURI

Address: 1F UF Bldg, 4-9-4 Roppongi, Minato-ku, Tokyo
How to get there: right by Exit 6 of Roppongi Station (Oedo Line)
Opening hours: daily, 11:00 to 09:00
Price: 1350 yen for the vegan ramen

This is one of the busier shops of the AFURI ramen chain, which offers one vegan ramen bowl. Find more information in the Nakameguro section of this guide. If the shop is full try the second Roppongi branch, which is in the basement of the nearby Roppongi Hills North Tower building.

.RAW

Address: 5-10-32 Roppongi, Minato, Tokyo
How to get there: from Exit 3 of Roppongi Station walk towards the right, then turn right again into a small sloping street right after the Almond café. Keep on following the street downwards. Eventually you should see the Step Roppongi building on your right. Continue on straight until you see a brown and white striped building on your left. The shop is in the next building, look for the sign and wheatgrass plants in the windows.
Opening hours: daily from 08:00 to 21:00.
Price: drinks around 700~800 yen, salad buffet 900~ 1100 yen and raw apple pie is 700 yen.

Whether or not you believe wheatgrass is a miracle cure, if you are looking for a quick fix of vegan, gluten free and raw nutrients, this covers all the bases. In addition to .RAW's famous fresh shots of wheatgrass, they also serve health food favorites like kombucha and apple/chia smoothies. The all-you-can-eat raw salad bar is a great deal for really fresh veggies, and if you take a morning yoga class you can get a discount on your meal. However, the reason I go back is for the excellent raw apple pie.

Shimokitazawa

Shimokitazawa is often compared to Brooklyn… at least by locals! A confusing warren of twisty streets with several small theaters, live houses, bookshops, galleries and dozens of coffee joints, "Shimo" is a cheerful mishmash that attracts lots of young, artistic folks. As with many parts of Tokyo, some of the best spots are tucked away in the side streets, and it can be a bit difficult to navigate, exacerbated by the expansion work they are doing on the station. The warren of bars which was once a main feature of the area has been stripped down to only a few remaining spots, in order to make room for the new station buildings, which is a pity and can cause some unpredictable changes in exits. Nonetheless, it is a great place to wander about while sipping a cup of coffee. Ex Libris is a particular favorite for coffee connoisseurs. The famous restaurant PolePole, one of the area's great vegan institutions, unfortunately closed in June 2017.

Chabuzen

Address: 6-16-2 Daita, Setagaya-ku, Tokyo
How to get there: take West Exit 1 of Shimokitazawa Station and take an immediate right (away from the train tracks). Keep going straight on this road for about 5 minutes, eventually you will pass the large white Seitoku school building on your left. Keep on going until you reach a small intersection and take a left right before a tiny park/sitting area. You will eventually pass a school, and the shop will be a little past the school on your right. It is very unassuming place, so keep an eye out.
Opening hours: open daily except Tuesdays, 12:00 to 15:00 and 17:00 to 23:00.
Price: 700~900 yen for curries and ramen, 200~600 yen for side dishes

This may well be not only one of the smallest vegan restaurants in Tokyo, but also one of the most overlooked. The owner is very open to visitors from abroad, and is a big fan of brown rice yeast and *yakuzen*, traditional medicinal herbs. But don't think that the hippy-ness of the ingredients has any negative effect on the food, which is all quite tasty, oriental-vegan friendly and a bit offbeat. One of the high points is the little fresh salads, which veer toward Indonesian flavors and have lots of interesting herbs mixed in. Another star is the rare vegan *oden*; a winter favorite, various ingredients simmered whole in stock. The ramen bowls are light and topped with more herbs, and the curries are surprisingly complex, even when they contain no garlic or onions. In summer don't miss the *hiyashi chuka*, cold noodles in a sweet/sour vinegar based sauce, covered with beautifully chopped veggies.

Yoyogi Area

The Yoyogi area of Tokyo can be a bit confusing, as it extends from Yoyogi Park (right by Harajuku Station) all the way to Yoyogi Uehara Station, several kilometers away. Most of the Yoyogi area is residential, filled with designer homes, trendy little restaurants and tiny expensive boutiques. Nearby Yoyogi Uehara Station you can find the beautiful Tokyo Camii mosque and Turkish cultural center, which is open daily for prayers and welcoming to visitors who wish to admire the lovely blue and white prayer hall.

This is also a good area for accommodation, as you get the benefit of being very close to the major areas of Harajuku/Omotesando, Shibuya and Shinjuku without the busyness and noise. Yoyogi Uehara also happens to be home to one of Tokyo's most unique vegan-friendly gourmet restaurants, as well as one of the city's great Japanese sweet shops (discussed more in depth in the Sweets and Treats section of this guide).

Tudore Tranquility

Address: 2-6-16 Uehara, Shibuya-ku, Tokyo
How to get there: hidden away on a side street, this is one case where having GPS would be helpful. From Yoyogi-Uehara Station, take either of the South Exits and go right. Keep walking straight until the road ends, and take a left. You should see the broad Inokashira Dori street in front of you. Cross the street and go left, following the large road. Walk for about 5 minutes, until the first street on your right (look for the green street lamps). Turn right into this smaller street, and go straight. You will then take the first left (right after a Domino's Pizza) into a small street. Follow it all the way down, and go down the stairs. Once you reach the road, take a left and walk straight for a few minutes. The restaurant will be on your right, look for the sign and white house.

Opening hours: open for dinner from Wednesday to Sunday, starting times 19:00~21:00. Reserve at least a couple days in advance from their website.
Price: eight-course dinner is around 13000 yen per person, wines starting around 6000 yen per bottle.

Dining at Tudore Tranquility feels a bit like being invited to a dinner party at the home of a world-class chef, quickly followed by being transported to another planet. From the reservation process, where you are considerately asked if there are any foods you dislike, to the service and chance to chat with chef Mamta Reid, the two hour course flies by, one carefully prepared dish at a time; a robust pilaf of black quinoa, vegan parmesan and tarragon 'butter', an addictive curry-filled flatbread with spiced soy beans, palate cleansers of cashew mozzarella and ephemeral pineapple mousse, all rounded out by a platter of desserts so indulgent you are likely to be struck silent. It is quite a ride, and definitely a great spot for a romantic occasion. Do specify when reserving that you are vegan, as the standard courses are vegetarian, and feel free to ask anything to the kind English-speaking staff.

Other Options in the Yoyogi Area

Bojun Tomigaya

Address: 2F Tomigaya Springs, 1-35-20 Tomigaya, Shibuya-ku, Tokyo
How to get there: from Yoyogikoen Station's Hachiman Exit (Exit 1), walk towards the left until you are in front of the Maruman grocery store. Across the street there is a small road, walk down this little road and take the first right. You will see a flight of stairs, climb up until you are right in front of a major road. Go to the left until you see a light-blue overhead pedestrian pass. Cross using the overhead pass, while staying on the same side. The restaurant is in the building on your left, look for the blue signs on the second floor.
Opening hours: daily except Mondays from 11:30~ 23:00 (last order 22:15).

Price: vegan options around 900~1300 yen, desserts 400~1100 yen.

A good option for a quick lunch, Bojun offers a small variety of standard vegan-friendly bowls and macrobiotic sets, which usually are based around herb-filled curries, veggie-meat croquettes and deli options. There is always one gluten free friendly dish and many of the desserts are both vegan and gluten free, including the refreshing strawberry mousse cake. Menus are available in English, and this restaurant is also quite welcoming for families, as they even have a vegan child plate.

Ikebukuro

Home to lots of cheap hotels and shopping spots, Ikebukuro also boasts Tokyo's second busiest station. This is a popular place to depart from to nearby Saitama prefecture, in particular to the charming town of Kawagoe, famous for its traditional buildings and yummy sweet potatoes.

Ikebukuro is also an interesting place to check out a different side of Japan's subculture. On Otome Road (literally Maiden Road) you can browse *manga* comic book shops, cosplay stores and cafés dedicated to female anime and *manga* fans. You can also find the (in)famous Swallowtail butler café, where one can be swept away to a fantasy world filled with butlers and tea. Vegetarians can be accommodated, but sadly there are no vegan options.

Nearby, the towering Sunshine City is a complex with tons of shopping options as well as small indoor amusement parks such as Namja Town. You can visit the wonderfully kitschy haunted house. At J-World Tokyo you can try out rides based on popular manga like Dragon Ball Z, Naruto and One Piece. Those who aren't keen on anime should check out the Manten Planetarium, where you can book special 'grass' and 'cloud' seats to lounge on as you gaze at the stars or special shows.

Senjyo Teuchi Gyoza Senmonten

Address: 2-55-12 Ikebukuro, Toshima, Tokyo
How to get there: from Exit C6 of Ikebukuro Station (Marunouchi Line), take a left onto a large street. Go straight until the intersection. Cross the road and continue straight on, taking the first left. You will pass the Sakura Hotel on your left. Keep going straight then take the next right. The shop will be on your left, look for the yellow sign with the following characters: 線條 手打餃子專門店
Opening hours: daily from 11:00 to 22:00, except Sundays when they open at 13:00.
Price: 750~1000 yen for a set meal, and 500 yen per plate of potstickers

The name of this tiny hole-in-the-wall may seem intimidating, but it basically boils down to 'potsticker specialist'. The chirpy Taiwanese lady who runs it provides a mind-boggling variety of different *gyoza*. Two kinds are vegan, and there is also a small selection of other oriental vegan dishes, including surprisingly realistic 'chicken' drumsticks. While you can opt for a potsticker set meal, which comes with rice, soup and one or two veggie side dishes, just ordering a few plates of *gyoza* is equally satisfying. Filled with unusual Chinese veggies such as lily root and fried in olive oil, they are lighter and more complex than one would expect. Cheap and cheerful, if a bit hard to find.

Other Options in Ikebukuro

Ain Soph Soar

Address: 1F Union Bldg, 3-5-7 Higashi-Ikebukuro, Toshima-ku, Tokyo
How to get there: from JR Ikebukuro Station, take the East Exit and cross the street on the wide crosswalk right in front of you. Towards the left you will see Sunshine Street (look for the old-fashioned street lamps). Take this road and walk all the way down for about 5 minutes, until you come to a highway with an overpass. Take a

right and then cross the large road at the crosswalk on your left. Once you are on the other side go left following the large road, just past the ARK hotel you will find the restaurant.

Opening hours: open daily, lunch is from 11:30 to 16:00 (last order 15:00) and dinner 17:00 to 22:00 (last order 21:00). On Sundays and holidays they also offer tea time between 15:00 to 17:00.

Price: 1100~1600 yen for lunch (on weekends prices go up by another 300 yen or so), budget around 3500~4000 yen for dinner.

The famous seasonal gluten free pancakes, colorful sandwiches and vegan version of *hayashi rice* (a Japanese beef and onion stew reminiscent of a thick demi-glace sauce, usually served with rice) are the main draw at this branch of the Ain Soph chain. Going on a weekday afternoon is recommended, as on weekends the prices go up and the lines can get quite long.

Off the Beaten Track

There are plenty of vegan-friendly restaurants and cafés around Tokyo, but many do tend to be located in areas that, while interesting in their own way, do not have any famous sights which call visitors to the capital. However, if you are looking to see a more local side of Tokyo, the top-notch food and cute, quiet neighborhoods are worth the train ride.

The Toyoko Line, Hibiya Line and Chuo Line seem to be popular congregation spots for plant-based cafés and restaurants, making it possible to hop from one to the other while exploring. For each area off the beaten track I have also included a bit of information about nearby sights and more famous spots on the same train line, so that you can plan your outings with ease.

Hiroo

With lots of embassies, wealthy expats and being quite close to pricy Roppongi and Azabu Juban, Hiroo is a ritzy neighborhood where English can be heard all around. Also home to the New Sanno Hotel, owned by the U.S. military, the area has a rather nice shopping street with some charming stores. Check out the fancy chopstick boutique and a spot that specializes in gourmet french fries, along with a small temple. Arisugawa-no-miya Park is right near the station, which has some good fall foliage, decent cherry blossoms and a few ponds with ducks and turtles. In the neighborhood you will also find the Natural Mart and National Azabu food store, as well as a large Natural Lawson, which all have excellent vegan snacks.

Hiroo is accessible from Hiroo Station on the Hibiya Line. It is just one stop away from both Roppongi and Ebisu, and five stops away from Ginza on the same line.

Trueberry

Address: 5-4-18 Hiroo, Shibuya-ku, Tokyo
How to get there: hidden in a side street very close to Hiroo Station's Exit 2. From the exit take a right into a shopping street, at the first side street look for the Trueberry sign and follow it into the tiny back street.
Opening hours: daily from 08:00 to 19:30
Price: 800 yen and up for a smoothie, 1000~1500 yen for a meal.

If you are craving a thick chocolate shake, but also want it to be vegan, gluten free and raw, then Trueberry is the place to go. A truly miniature shop, you will never be more than a few feet away from the blenders that whip up the smoothies, cold-pressed juices and frozen concoctions which are their specialty. From spirulina-laced green smoothies– which can also be served hot, should you be so inclined– to surprisingly decadent frappucino-esque creations featuring raw cocoa, matcha and blended cashews, the drink menu is quite large. The food options are more limited, with raw sandwiches, curries, brown rice and a selection of raw desserts.

Vegan Cafe

Address: Urban Hiroo 1F, 4-5-65 Minamiazabu, Minato-ku, Tokyo
How to get there: from Exit 1 of Hiroo Station take an immediate left and cross the street. Go left again and walk straight for about 1 minute, you should see the building right in front of you.
Opening hours: daily 10:00 to 21:00 (last order 20:00)
Price: 1000~1800 yen for a meal, desserts starting from 400 yen

Although the straightforward name of this minimal spot may lack in creativity, the amusingly spelled English menu, chatty owner and unique dishes have already made this a fashionable spot for expats to hang out. The menu is small but covers a lot of ground, featuring unusual dishes like stuffed baguettes, Hawaiian-style loco moco bowls, gluten free pasta and even a colorful paella. However, one of the most interesting choices has to be the vegan sushi, which includes an impressive red pepper 'tuna' and a rendition of squid crafted from aloe. A newcomer to Tokyo's vegan scene, it is clear they are still finding their feet, but I expect their menu will bloom with time.

Jimbocho

In the book seller's district around the station, there are dozens of used book stores, each with its own specialty, ranging from cooking to Chinese classical literature and everything in between. Unsurprisingly almost all of the books are in Japanese, but Kitazawa Books (located right outside the A1 Exit of Jimbocho Station) has a good selection of English books. Other good places to check out are Yamada Shoten, which specializes in *ukiyoe* woodblock prints and other Japanese prints for very affordable prices, and Sinsendo, which has a huge selection of vintage and antique maps from all over the world. On a rainy day check out the shops, then crack open your new book and read for a bit at Koseto, a colorful café and gallery. You can walk or take a train to Kudanshita, where you will find Yasukuni Shrine, the National Showa Memorial Museum and Chidorigafuchi, a section of moat lined with cherry blossoms during the spring.

Jimbocho can be accessed from Jimbocho Station, which is on the Mita, Shinjuku and Hanzomon Lines. On the Mita line it is just a few stop away from Meguro as well as Sugamo, which has a lively shopping street, known as the 'Harajuku of the Elderly', and lots of little temples to explore. The Shinjuku line obviously connects it to Shinjuku as well as nearby Kudanshita. The Hanzomon line can take you to Shibuya and Omotesando one way, or in the opposite direction to Oshiage, right by the Skytree.

Loving Hut

Address: Okada Bldg 2F, 1-54, Jimbocho, Kanda, Chiyoda-ku, Tokyo
How to get there: from Exit A5 of Jimbocho Station turn the corner on the right and walk straight. Turn into the ninth street on your right, and you will see the sign.
Opening hours: only open on Saturdays, lunch buffet is from 11:00 to 15:00 and dinner from 17:00 to 20:30. Sometimes they are away for veggie-related events, check via Twitter to be on the safe side.
Price: 600~1500 yen for a meal, depending on size, 1500 yen for the buffet.

The Tokyo branch of a large Asian vegan chain, this is the place to go for a fully vegan brunch on Saturdays. Starting with dim sum, including the justly famous jumbo *gyoza*, moving on to stir-fries and faux-meat skewers and finishing with noodle dishes and fresh fruit, even the largest appetite can be tamed here. For dinner, the *kabayaki* grilled 'eel' is one of the musts, with a convincing springiness and sauce with just the right degree of sweetness. You can also call in advance to order the 5-piece veggie sushi set. There are plenty of gluten free options as well, including several of their best dishes. Note that the Loving Hut franchise is run by an odd, if relatively innocuous spiritual group, so the atmosphere is not exactly scintillating and the weird musical playing in the background just has to be ignored. But for this price it is worth the effort.

Okubo

Traditionally the 'Koreatown' of Tokyo, during the height of the Korean Wave this spot was overflowing with visitors looking to stock up on Korean make-up, photos of K-pop stars and yummy street food like *toppoki* and *chijimi*. As the Korean boom has mostly ended, new nationalities are moving into the Hyakunincho area, and there has been an influx of Muslim-friendly businesses providing halal restaurants, markets (the most famous being Nasco Halal Food and Jannat) and even a tiny mosque! As Tokyo doesn't really have a Chinatown area, this is the closest equivalent.

Okubo can be accessed from both Okubo and Shin Okubo Station. Okubo Station is on the Chuo Line, just one stop away from Shinjuku. Two stops away is Nakano, home to Nakano Broadway, an indoor shopping arcade with a mind boggling number of stores dedicated anime/manga and other interesting parts of Japan's subculture. Make sure to check out the retro sci-fi toys at Mandarake. A longer ride will take you to Kichijoji, known for Inokashira Park and Mitaka, which is where the magical Ghibli Museum is located. If you want to visit the museum, make sure you get tickets at least a couple months in advance.

Shin Okubo Station is on the Yamanote line, between Shinjuku and Ikebukuro. The two stations are only 300 meters apart, which can be helpful depending on your next destination.

Saishokukenbi

Address: 2-21-26 Hyakunin-cho, Shinjuku-ku, Tokyo
How to get there: from Okubo Station's North Exit, cross the street and walk down the large street (Okubo Dori) towards the right. You should see a Seven Eleven convenience store on your left. Take the second street to the left, and walk until you see the temple with the giant Buddha. Go into the courtyard, the restaurant is in the main building.
Opening hours: open daily except for Tuesdays, from 11:00 to 15:00.
Price: from 780~1300 yen.

The Tokyo branch of a small chain owned by the Dotoku-Kaikan spiritual group, the large menu of this oriental vegetarian/vegan spot is rather impressive. Although some of the dishes include dairy or eggs (just tell the staff you are vegan and they will be happy to point out which dishes to avoid), the Taiwanese-style faux meats, dim sum and very reasonable prices make it worth a visit for lunch. The vegan eel is nicely grilled, presented beautifully in the traditional lacquered box, and suffused with the savory-sweet *kabayaki* sauce which makes this dish so appealing. The array of fried cutlets, skewers and steamed *gyoza*, as well as rice bowls with toppings such as spicy Chinese-style tofu or soy meat and kimchi, have plenty of heft. This is a great spot to check out with a small group, so that you can share and try several of the specialties. No alcohol is served, so just stick to tea or juices, as the coffee is predictably uninspiring. Towards the entrance you will find a small selection of packaged foods, as well as a few drinks and sweets available for purchase.

<u>Ebisu</u>

Right within walking distance of Shibuya, Daikanyama, Nakameguro and Hiroo, Ebisu is easy to get to and known as one of the top well-heeled neighborhoods of Tokyo, with lots of shopping, cafés and Ebisu Garden Place. Named after the Ebisu brewery, which used to be located here, you can visit the Museum of Yebisu beer and try some samples for under 500 yen. Take a quick stroll around the Ebisu Garden Place area to check out the incongruous Joel Robuchon restaurant, which looks like a small castle. During the Christmas season the entire area becomes a hot date spot, with lots of couples coming to see a giant Baccarat crystal chandelier lit up after dark.

Art lovers will like the area for its multitude of small galleries, such as the Tokyo Metropolitan Museum of Photography with its rotating exhibits, as well as the bijou Yamatane Museum of Art's Japanese paintings and the eclectic Matsuoka Museum of Art.

If you are looking for an evening out, Ebisu is an excellent choice with hundreds of restaurants and bars to choose from. Ebisu Yokocho is a charming spot to get a feel for Japanese *izakaya* pub culture. This 'indoor alleyway' has a selection of tiny little bars crammed together for a bit of festive chaos, great for bar hopping without getting wet on rainy days.

Ebisu is accessible from Ebisu Station, which is one stop away from Shibuya on the JR Yamanote Line. If you are traveling with the JR pass this train line will be your major artery around the city. It is just a couple stops away from Roppongi on the Hibiya Line, which can also take you to the tech and anime hub of Akihabara. Alternatively head over to Ueno, where Ueno Park has lots of temples, historical museums, statues and seasonal flowers to enjoy.

KO-SO CAFE

Address: Lions Plaza Ebisu 1F, 3-25-3 Higashi, Shibuya-ku, Tokyo
How to get there: standing with your back to the ticket gates of the West Exit of JR Ebisu Station take a right (you should see a Montbell store), then take a left onto the small road. Once you reach the large Komazawa Dori street take a right again, and

cross at the first cross walk on your left. Right in front of you there will be a smaller road between two large buildings (one is white with a vertical strip of windows). Go straight, and you will find the café on the left side, look for the green sign.
Opening hours: open daily, weekdays from 11:00 to 21:30 (last order 21:00), weekends and holidays 11:30 to 20:00 (last order 19:00).
Price: 1000~1500 yen for lunch, budget 2000~3000 yen for dinner. Pancakes around 880~1400 yen.

Literally translated as 'enzyme café', this colorful little restaurant sneaks brown rice and a fermented 'enzyme paste' made with 88 different veggies into most of their dishes. Although it sounds a bit odd, it may well be the secret to the complex flavors the chefs whip up with aplomb. The café is mainly famous for their colorful vegan pancakes, in particular the cocoa-scented 'detox pancakes', however the large selection of seasonal dishes should not be underestimated. The vegan pizza's brown rice crust serves as a base for a well-balanced combination of punchy tomato sauce and creamy 'cheese', and recent starters of stuffed mini green peppers and taro root nuggets with cilantro had heft and umami to spare. Be aware that the pasta sauces are Japanese-style, so they tend to be soupier than one would expect from Italian cuisine. KO-SO is certified halal and vegan, and has quite a few gluten free options on their menu, including 100% buckwheat pancakes.

Rainbow Raw Food/ Hemp Café

Address: 3-17-14-8F Higashi, Shibuya-ku, Tokyo, Japan
How to get there: follow the instructions to get to KO-SO CAFE. Once you pass it, turn right before the 'cracked' building. Go to the end of the little street and the building will be right in front of you, the restaurant is on the eighth floor.
Opening hours: open for lunch Tuesday through Saturday from 11:30 to 15:30 (last order at 14:30). Dinner available Monday through Saturday from 17:00 to 23:00 (last order at 22:00).

Price: 1350~1500 yen for lunch, budget 2000~3000 yen for dinner. Course meals available by reservation.

Say aloha to one of Tokyo's oldest raw food joints! Rainbow Raw has been around since 2010, an amazing feat in a city with such quick turnaround for niche restaurants. The modest menu features dishes such as raw sushi rolls, a creamy version of pad thai and burritos with a good kick of Tex Mex spice and vegan sour cream. Portions are not huge, which is just as well since you absolutely want to leave room for dessert. The cashew nut based cheesecake could fool non-vegans, and their brownie combines cocoa with rum-raisin to good effect. The owner lived and trained in the U.S., so this is a very English-friendly place and a good introduction to raw food for the uninitiated. Basically everything on the menu is also gluten free. During the evening it transforms into the Hemp Café, with a selection of vegan, raw and hemp-based dishes to try.

SUMI-BIO

Address: Ebisu First Place 2F, 1-22-8 Ebisu, Shibuya-ku, Tokyo
How to get there: from the East Exit of Ebisu Station, follow the road to the right, going down the hill. You will reach a crossroads. Staying towards the left, cross the road and take the smaller road that curves towards the left. It is in the third building on the second floor.
Opening hours: open daily, lunch from 11:30 to 15:00 (last order at 14:30) and dinner from 17:30 to 23:30 (last order 22:30).
Price: 900~1300 for lunch, around 3000 yen and up for dinner, more if you order wine.

With a polished wooden bar counter, chandeliers and private little tables, this organic restaurant is a great place for a special occasion or to take friends and family who are not vegan, as they do also serve meat dishes. Lunch is an excellent deal, with a selection of sets featuring Chinese dishes like spicy *mabo tofu* and *hoikoro* (a miso-based stir-fry). Dinner is more varied, and their seasonal specials focus around organic veggies they buy directly from nearby farmers. The pasta and risotto dishes are well-presented, and you will not want to miss the banana-tofu clafoutis if it is available. The staff doesn't speak English, but are familiar with veganism, so can point out which dishes are safe.

Other Options in Ebisu

AFURI

Address: 1F 117 Bldg, 1-1-7 Ebisu, Shibuya-ku, Tokyo
How to get there: from JR West Exit of Ebisu Station, go out towards the right. Walk towards the right, and then turn left before the McDonalds. Cross the street, and keep on going straight until you see a park. Go left, the shop is in the fourth building.
Opening hours: daily from 11:00 to 05:00.
Price: 1350 yen for the vegan ramen.

This is the original shop of the AFURI ramen chain, which has one vegan ramen bowl that can also be made with gluten free noodles. Find more information in the Nakameguro section of this guide.

Cosme Kitchen Adaptation

Address: Ebisu Atre West Bldg 2F, 1-6-1 Ebisuminami, Shibuya-ku, Tokyo
How to get there: from the East Exit of Ebisu Station near the roundabout, look to your left. You should see the Atre building immediately in front of you, the restaurant is on the 2nd floor.
Opening hours: daily from 10:00 to 23:00 (last order at 22:30).
Prices: between 1300~2000 yen.

The newest restaurant of the Cosme Kitchen beauty brand, this spot is a lifesaver if you have to deal with lots of dietary requirements, as they offer vegan, gluten free, raw and carnivorous options. One of the big draws is their 'clean eating' lunch buffet, which offers a huge range of colorful organic veggies, deli options, soups and cold-pressed dressings.

Make sure to leave room for the raw chocolate-raspberry tart or a fruity parfait. Best visited on weekdays, as you can expect to wait up to one hour to be seated during the weekend.

Dear My Body

Address: Ito Bldg B1F, 1-8-47 Ebisu, Shibuya-ku, Tokyo
How to get there: standing with your back to the ticket gates of the West Exit of JR Ebisu Station take the exit to the right, cross the street and go right again. Take a left at the street right after the white tiled building. The restaurant is in the third building on the left, look for the name on the planter box.
Opening hours: daily except Sundays from 12:00 to 16:00, dinner from 18:00 to 23:30 (last order 30 minutes before closing).
Prices: 1000~15000 yen for lunch, 2500~3000 yen for vegan or gluten free dinner courses.

An ideal spot for a quick healthy lunch, Dear My Body various daily lunch sets which are both vegan and gluten free. The taco rice is filling and has a nice fan of avocado wedges which adds a bit of weight to the dish, and the noodle dishes usually revolve around pho or other rice-based noodles, often topped with a savory 'meat' sauce and some crunchy veggies. The menu includes some non-vegan dishes, making it a useful spot for visitors looking for an omni option.

Daikanyama

Accessible from nearby Shibuya, Ebisu and Nakameguro, this neighborhood is a fashionable date spot, dotted with designer shops, interior design stores, more hair salons than one would think possible, interesting cafés and lots of very expensive housing. Sightseeing-wise, the Kyu Asakura house, built in 1919, is a wonderful example of combined Japanese and Western architecture, with a pleasant garden and spots to sit and gaze at it contemplatively. At Daikanyama T-Site you can explore the huge, artsy Tsutaya book store, which has a decent selection of English-language books and magazines, as well as a constantly changing range of crafts, foods, art and other intriguing things for sale. Beer lovers will want to check out the gorgeous Spring Valley Brewery in nearby LogRoad, which has seasonal craft beers and a wood and glass structure that feels like it could just take flight.

Daikanyama is on the Toyoko Line, just one stop away from Shibuya. Other close stations are Nakameguro, Gakugeidaigaku, Toristudaigaku and Jiyugaoka, which do not often feature in guidebooks but all have pleasant shopping streets, cafés, small parks and cherry-blossom lined roads, which can be nice for a look into the more 'local' side of Tokyo.

Blu Jam Cafe

Address: Mon-Cheri Building B2, 20-20 Daikanyama-cho, Shibuya-ku, Tokyo
How to get there: after exiting Daikanyama Station's Central Exit, take the road to the right (not the one going downhill). The restaurant is in the basement of the second large building on your right, look for the signboard.
Opening hours: open every day except Tuesdays between 08:00 to 22:00 (last order 21:00).
Price: around 1100~1500 per vegan dish. Vegetarian, gluten free and meat-based dishes are a bit more.

This all-day brunch joint opened in 2016, and quickly became a popular spot for U.S. expats looking to fulfill their Sunday morning cravings. As the menu is based off that of the original shop in Los Angeles, you will find no Japanese food here. However, the masterful vegan rancheros, with its well-spiced blackened tofu scramble set on a bed of tiny crunchy potatoes alone makes it worth a visit. The English menu and fluent English-speaking staff make ordering a breeze, with all vegan, vegetarian and gluten free options clearly marked.

Other Options in Daikanyama

Crisp Salad Works

Address: 2F Daikanyama Plaza, 24-7 Sarugakucho, Shibuya-ku, Tokyo
How to get there: located in the building across the street from Blu Jam Cafe, on the second floor.
Opening hours: daily between 11:00 to 22:00.
Price: expect around 1000~1500 yen for a made-to-order salad.

This American-style chopped salad joint also has branches in Roppongi, Azabu Juban, Hiroo and Ebisu. While not unique, the clear English, detailed labeling and large selection of vegan and gluten free toppings and dressings make this a reliable standby for a quick lunch or a leafy snack. The Earthy Nutty Crunchy salad is particularly good thanks to the lemony tahini dressing which adds a refreshing kick.

Jiyugaoka

A little out of central Tokyo, Jiyugaoka is considered a chic spot to live and is thus filled with little boutiques, fancy cafés and elegant houses. While not a major center for sightseeing, in spring the cherry blossoms are in full bloom on the main shopping street. Not far from the station the La Vita complex recreates a tiny bit of Venice (complete with canals and even a gondola). Right across the street you will find Kosouan, a lovely teahouse which was once the home of the daughter of Natsume Soseki, one of Japan's most famous writers. There are lots of little streets to explore and a few unobtrusive shrines and temples. While finding interesting shops is no problem in this area, just off the main tree-lined street Katakana specializes in really cute household goods, food items and clothing made in Japan.

Another offbeat location to check out is the Jiyugaoka Department Store which, despite the name, resembles more of a retro indoor bazaar. The entrance is right by the Central Exit of Jiyugaoka Station. Look to the right, it is the unassuming entrance with kitchenware stacked nearby. The long, narrow corridors are lined with all sorts of oddities. Kimono shops adjoin pickled veggie stores, antique jewelry and household ceramics, beauty products and anything else you could think of, making for an eclectic atmosphere. The basement is equally intriguing.

Jiyugaoka Station is on the Toyoko Line, making it an easy side trip from Shibuya and Nakameguro, or a good place to stop on the way to or from Yokohama.

T's Restaurant

Address: Luz Jiyugaoka Bldg, 2-2-9-6 Jiyugaoka, Meguro-ku, Tokyo
How to get there: from the Central Exit of Jiyugaoka Station, take the third street on your right. Keep going straight, and look for the Luz building on your left. The restaurant is in the basement.
Opening hours: daily 11:00 to 22:00 (last order 21:00).
Price: 1350~1500 yen for lunch, around 2500~3000 yen for dinner, tea time cakes around 600~700 yen.

A personal favorite, a meal at T's is always a pleasure. The sheer luxury of choice and the presence of comfort food such as lasagna and *doria* (a creamy rice gratin) on the menu are two reasons why this restaurant has such an important place in the heart of most Tokyo vegans. While everything they whip up in the open kitchen is great, there are a few standout dishes. The *yurinchi karaage*, fried 'chicken' tossed in a savory, vinegary Chinese sauce, is a perfect prelude to the creamy, bubbly lasagna or their incredible *tantanmen*- spicy ramen with minced 'meat', one of their signature dishes. For dessert a ramekin of creme caramel or pound cake topped with berries is perfect. The only thing that mars the excellence of this spot is the coffee, which is bland. Opt for one of the berry or herb cordials instead, which are particularly nice during the hot summer months. Find out about their ramen shop in the Tokyo Station portion of this guide.

Shiro

Address: 2-9-14 Jiyugaoka, Meguro-ku, Tokyo
How to get there: from the Central Exit of Jiyugaoka Station, take the third street to your right. Walk until the crossroad, then take a left. Go straight until the next crossroad, and turn right. You will see the café's sign straight ahead.
Opening hours: daily from 10:00 to 20:00.
Price: meals 1000~1600 yen, parfaits are 1400 yen.

Run by a natural cosmetics company, Shiro has become a popular brunch spot among fashionable Japanese women, making it a great spot for people watching. The menu is entirely vegan and clearly caters to their predominantly female patrons, with excellent fluffy pancakes and highly photogenic—and delicious—parfaits made with coconut and soy milk ice cream. The savory side of the menu can be a little more hit or miss. Their vegan curry, served on a sizzling hot plate and topped with plenty of colorful veggies and 'cheese' is filling, while the soup and rice balls set is a good option if you want to leave more room for dessert. While the cosmetics for sale smell heavenly unfortunately they are not vegan, so keep that in mind before going on a shopping spree.

Nakameguro

Strung along the Meguro River, this classy neighborhood is a favorite spot of Japanese celebrities, wealthy expats and ladies who lunch with small fluffy dogs in tow. The entire river, which extends all the way to Gotanda and Osaki, is lined with huge old cherry trees, making it a very popular spot in spring. In winter the same trees are decked out with fairy lights, for a romantic evening stroll, and in the summer the tree cover makes it cooler than the rest of the sweltering city. Off the main drag there are a few cute *shoutengai* (traditional shopping streets) and the small Sato Sakura Museum of Art, dedicated to various depictions of cherry blossoms. Jaho Coffee, the Tokyo branch of a Boston coffee chain, is a good spot to stop for a caffeine break and people watching. Vegetarians will want to check out Potager, a patisserie that uses veggies to create their desserts. Avocado cheesecake or burdock chocolate cake anyone?

Nakameguro Station is on both the Hibiya and Toyoko lines, and is just two stops away from Shibuya.

Rainbow Bird Rendevous

Address: 1F Liberta Yutenji Bldg, 1-1-1 Yutenji, Meguro-ku, Tokyo
How to get there: it is about a 10 minute walk from Nakameguro Station, but easy to find. Go out the Main Gate of Nakameguro Station, and turn right. Pass a large building, and take another right between the building and the Tsutaya. Then just keep going straight down the shopping street until you see the café right in front of you.

Opening hours: weekdays except Wednesday, lunch 11:30 to 16:00 and dinner 17:30 to 20:00. Saturdays 11:30 to 20:00, Sundays and holidays 11:30 to 19:00.
Price: 880~1550 yen for lunch and a bit more for dinner, smoothies from 600 yen and desserts from 510 yen and up.

Cute and homey, RBR is located on a little shopping street a bit off the beaten track. The fare is simple, with staples such as soy meat hamburgers, comforting potato croquettes and big salads appearing regularly, along with the daily specials which are often served with *onigiri* rice balls. Although the desserts change seasonally, the gluten free, raw chocolate cake and baked lemon 'cheesecake' are worth a stop for an afternoon treat. They also serve a good version of vegan soft serve ice cream, made with nuts and maple syrup. The staff speaks English and the menus are written in English, a nice surprise in such a tiny spot.

AFURI

Address: 1F Nakameguro Arena, 1-23-1 Kamimeguro, Meguro-ku, Tokyo
How to get there: after exiting the Main Exit of Nakameguro Station, immediately cross the street. The restaurant is on the first floor in the first large building on your right.
Opening hours: daily, 11:00 to 05:00.
Price: 1,350 yen for the vegan ramen.

A relative rarity in the down-and-dirty world of ramen, Afuri tends towards lighter, almost 'refreshing' ramen, which is served in airy, trendy, chrome filled spaces, creating an unusually hipsterish ramen experience. While most of their menu is based around their chicken oil broth, they have one 100% vegan bowl available at all times. The Seasonal Vegan Ramen is topped with vegetables from nearby Kamakura, and as the name suggests the veggies are the best selection for that week. The broth is light and almost Italianate, with the thin noodles resting in an olive oil, garlic and red-pepper laced broth. Opt for an extra dish of *nori* (dried seaweed) to add another layer of flavor to this unusual noodle dish. Open until 5 in the morning, this chain is a lifesaver after a night out, and has several branches across the city.

Ogikubo and Nishi Ogikubo Area

Way off the beaten path, Nishi Ogi, as it is known by its fans, is much quieter and more restful than either of its neighboring stations. The three long shopping streets, cute shops and tons of vintage/antique stores make it worth a stop on your way to the Ghibli Museum or Inokashira Park. Sake fans will want to make a pilgrimage to Mitsuya Saketen, a huge sake emporium with bottles of rice wine from all across Japan, which is right on the way from the station to Trim. It is also something of a vegan hotspot, with a few excellent must-tries. Ogikubo is just one station over and is much busier, although nearby Otaguro Park and the 'weeping' *jizo* statue at Komyoin Temple are well-worth a visit.

Ogikubo and Nishiogikubo are just a couple stops from Kichijoji Station on the Chuo Line, and are also close to Koenji.

Komenoko

Address: Tokyo, Suginami-ku, Nishiogikita 3-25-1 Shippo Mansion 1F
How to get there: take the North Exit of Nishi Ogikubo Station, and follow the road to the left. At the third crossroads (by the bakery) take a right. It is the small shop with a white and black sign and glass doors.
Opening hours: daily except Thursdays, lunch from 11:30 to 15:00, dinner 18:00 to 21:00.
Price: 1100 for a set meal, 300~700 yen for extra sides, and a few hundred yen more for drinks with the sets.

As the restaurant's name means 'rice child', it is not surprising the owner focuses the small menu around perfectly steamed rice from Akita prefecture and fresh veggies, both organic and pesticide-free. While occasionally there are some changes to the menu for holidays, in general you have the option of a lovely tray with a main dish, two or three veggies sides, rice and a refreshingly subtle, veggie-filled miso soup. The mains are robust *gyoza* potstickers, savory and complex lotus root based patties, fried 'chicken' or simple grilled veggies. The sides usually vary depending on the main dish chosen, and are bright, well-balanced examples of Japanese home cooking.

You can order smaller versions of the main dishes on the side, should you wish to sample more than one, a nice touch. The dark wooden interior, glass door overhung with plants and quiet atmosphere make it a relaxing spot. The English menu makes ordering simple. Desserts tend towards Japanese favorites, often jellies. The chocolate ice cream is reliably good, if portioned out a tad stingily. Visitors with a sweet tooth might want to swing by Trim afterwards.

Trim

Address: Lion's Mansion 1F, 1-19-20 Nishiogikubo, Suginami-ku, Tokyo
How to get there: from the South Exit of Nishi Ogikubo Station, take either of the little streets that start right in front of the exit. Once the little street ends turn left onto the larger road and just keep walking straight for about 10 minutes, keeping an eye out on your right for the white sign and the brown-tiled building.
Opening hours: daily except Mondays from 12:00 to 19:00 (last order 18:30).
Price: lunch 1000~1200 yen, desserts and drinks in the 400~600 yen range.

A quiet white and gray haven, the sweets at Trim are much like the decor of this petite café: simple, homey and perfectly balanced. With a nice daily selection of cakes, muffins and even unusual vegan puddings, the seasonal desserts make this a must-try after lunch at Komenoko. Accompanied by a warming mug of soymilk chai or herb tea, you can spend a pleasant hour nibbling the fruity blueberry cake, lemon-infused muffins or robust chocolate cake. They also serve a fully vegan lunch, but as most of their clientele is female it can be a bit light. Offerings usually include soups, salads, veggie-based deli options and their savory muffins. Do keep in mind that it may take a while to receive your order, and that most of the menu is in Japanese, although the staff are happy to help.

Cafe Bask

Address: 2-30-16 Kamiogi, Suginami-ku, Tokyo
How to get there: from the South Exit of Ogikubo Station face the road and go right, following the train tracks. Go all the way down until you reach the end of the fence, then look to your left for the entrance to the underpass. Take this to get to the other side of the tracks, then take the road to the left. Ahead you will see a blue pedestrian overpass. Right after the overpass look for the café's orange sign.
Opening hours: daily, 12:00 to 23:30.
Price: 1200~2000 yen for a meal, desserts and drinks in the 400~600 yen range.

Vegan-friendly terrace bars are few and far between in Tokyo, which makes chilling on Bask's deck with a cold drink and selection of goodies a lovely way to spend an afternoon or summer evening. Their well-priced lunch plate special is the best way to sample a wide selection of all their deli dishes at once, which are made with fresh organic vegetables and tend to harmoniously fuse Japanese and Western flavors. The set always includes a standout main dish, such as a fried roulade of tofu, pickled plum and shiso leaves.

Leave room for the seasonal desserts, particularly if their luscious blueberry or apple pies are on the menu, or get a couple muffins to go.

Koenji Area

Famous for its vintage/second-hand clothing shops, colorful Awa Odori dance festival in August and long shopping streets, Koenji is a fun place to stay a little out of central Tokyo. As rent is cheaper than in central Tokyo this neighborhood attracts a young, artistic crowd, making it a great place for funky live music venues, bars and unusual little shops. Pal Street and Look Street, two of the covered shopping arcades, are particularly good if you are looking to score some vintage finds. This is where Lady Gaga apparently gets some of her over-the-top apparel! Photo and Instagram fans will find the little side streets, lit with lanterns and signs after dark, wonderfully atmospheric. While there are no major must-see temples or shrines, though you may find a few hidden here and there, it is a nice place to just browse and blend in a bit. There are quite a few expats who call it home.

Koenji Station is on the Chuo Line, just four stops away from Shinjuku, and right next to Nakano—described in more detail in the Okubo section of this guide. The second recommended restaurant is right by Higashi Koenji Station, which is on the Marunouchi Line a few stops away from Shinjuku.

vege&grain cafe meu nota

Address: 3-45-11-2F Koenjiminami, Suginami-ku, Tokyo
How to get there: take the South Exit of Koenji Station and go straight into the large covered shopping street straight ahead called Kounan Street. Walk through the shopping street and take the fourth right, right after the Safari used clothing store. Keep on going straight until you come to the Seiyu supermarket. Look to your left, on the second floor you should see the sign for meu nota.
Opening hours: open Wednesday through Sunday, lunch is from 12:00 to 15:30 (last order at 14:30) and dinner is from 17:30 to 22:30 (last order at 21:30). On

Wednesdays they are only open for dinner, and occasionally the hours may change due to music events.
Price: 880~1230 yen for lunch, budget at least 2000 yen for dinner.

Climbing up the steep little staircase and entering this retro-styled café may feel a bit like visiting a charming version of your grandmother's attic. This eatery features healthy plates of vegan cuisine. The reasonably priced lunch sets are filled with color and interesting tidbits, and the 30-ingredient taco-rice salad has a good punch of chili and lots of avocado for creaminess. The curries change daily, but the chef seems to have a weakness for Sri Lankan-style concoctions, which is unusual in Tokyo. Unsurprisingly, considering the name of the café, the dinner menu has a few standout salads which feature unusual grains and homemade dressings, and the vegan *bagna cauda* (a Northern Italian hot dip) may well be unique in Tokyo.

Kitchen Cocomo

Address: Kurashima Bldg 2F, 3-60-11 Wada, Suginami-ku, Tokyo
How to get there: from Higashi Koenji Station's Exit 2, take a left. Keep going straight, eventually passing a large pachinko parlor called Kotobuki on your left. Keep on going straight until you see a crosswalk. Cross the street and take a left, and just a little further ahead you should see Cocomo's colorful sign.
Opening hours: daily, lunch from 11:30 to 15:00, last order at 14:30. Dinner from 17:30 to 22:00, last order at 21:00.
Price: lunch from 1000~1560 yen, four-dish dinner courses starting from 2360 yen.

A wonderful little restaurant that is sadly not very good at promoting itself, Cocomo is run by an experienced team of vegetarian and vegan chefs, and their talent shines through in all their dishes. Curry is usually not the highlight of most vegan restaurant menus, but the double curry set—which comes with a smooth Japanese-style curry, punchy *keema* and a dollop of coriander sauce—is flavorful and complex, especially decadent when topped with a vegan cutlet. The avocado and balsamic vinegar-infused tartare, pasta with truffle sauce and desserts are also impressive, as is the fact they serve good Italian Illy coffee. Note that the menu is currently only in Japanese with vegan dishes marked with a 'V', so if you are unsure ask the staff for help.

Kichijoji

Constantly ranked as one of the most desirable places to live in Tokyo, this chichi suburb of the capital is just a quick train ride away. Although it used to be more similar to Koenji with an artistic and hip vibe, Kichijoji is now edging closer to trendy and fashionable.

The first must-see out here is Inokashira Park, a large park surrounding a lake filled with swan boats. But watch out, urban legend has it that couples who paddle in one of these romantic boats together will break up! If you feel up to it, rent one of the little boats during the spring or autumn, for great views and the opportunity to float under the seasonal colors. This park is gorgeous during cherry blossom season.

Follow the signs that will take you on a pleasant walk to the area's second claim to fame, the Ghibli Museum. Even if you aren't a big fan of Miyazaki's animations, this is still a beautiful, immersive little museum, and requires booking tickets in advance. The Straw Hat Café' attached to the museum is all-organic but unfortunately, with the exception of the refreshing homemade ginger ale, nothing appears to be vegan.

Kichijoji Station is on both the Chuo Line and the Inokashira Line. For other places to check out on the Chuo Line take a look at the information available above. The Inokashira Line connects you directly to Shibuya, and on the way you will find Shimokitazawa, considered the 'Brooklyn of Tokyo'.

Monk's Foods

Address: 1-2-4 Gotenyama, Musashino, Tokyo
How to get there: from the North Exit of Kichijoji Station, take an immediate left and go straight (keeping the station on your left) until you reach a large intersection. Cross at the crosswalk right in front of you (you should be able to see the entrance to Nakamichi street) and then take another left. Pass under the bridge and keep going straight across the crosswalk. Pass the Step in Step on your right, and follow the road straight ahead. You will cross straight through another small crosswalk, and about 50 meters ahead on the right you will find it. Look for the dark wood front with white script.
Opening hours: daily except Wednesdays. Weekdays from 11:30 to 22:30 (last order 22:00) and weekends and national holidays from 11:30 to 21:30 (last order 21:00)
Price: 900~1080 yen

This simple, down-to-earth restaurant has been around since 1983, weathering the mercurial nature of Kichijoji real estate. Every day, the jazz-loving owner dreams up three set menus created with seasonal organic ingredients, one of which is always vegan. The cuisine is traditional Japanese fare based around the *ichiju sansai* (one soup and three sides) principle, so you will get three veggie dishes, miso soup and a bowl of rice. Due to the seasonal and ever-changing nature of the menu it is hard to tell what you will be served, but if you are lucky enough to get one of the pumpkin *nimono* stewed dishes or fresh tofu stir-fry you are in for a treat. The owner can speak some English and is careful about checking food preferences for guests who order the vegetable set menus.

Yanaka/Nezu/Sendagi

Commonly known as YaNeSen, the triangle created by the neighborhoods of Yanaka, Nezu and Sendagi is one of the most charmingly old school spots in Tokyo. Left relatively unscathed by the bombing during WW2, the twisty temple-lined streets and old-fashioned wooden buildings are reminiscent of Kyoto. Just out the North Exit of Nippori Station you will find the tranquil Yanaka Cemetery and Tennoji Temple. Crafters and textile-lovers should check out 'Fabric Town' just a few minutes from the South Exit.

Yanaka Ginza, the main shopping street just a few minutes away from the North Exit, has a fun retro vibe, and you may be able to see some of the famous local kitties being fussed over by camera-wielding ladies. If you want to try *kakigori* (a shaved ice dessert with flavored syrups or fruit, mostly vegan) Himitsudo is a good option, very popular during Tokyo's hot summers. At SCAI The Bathhouse you can check out modern art housed in a former public bath. Wander in the direction of Nezu Station, and enjoy getting a bit lost in the twisty streets. Nezu Shrine is a lovely spot with a long row of orange torii gates and a hill of bright azaleas that bloom from April to early May. While there are plenty of fun shops, paper enthusiasts should absolutely pass by Isetatsu, where you can find colorful Edo-style prints and handmade paper.

Yanaka can be accessed from Nippori Station on the Yamanote Line. It is just two stops away from Ueno and two stops away from Komagome, which is where the Rikugien Garden is located. Although walking from Yanaka to Nezu is recommended, if you are coming from a different direction Nezu Station is on the Chiyoda Line, four stops away from Nijubashimae (the closest station to the Imperial Palace and Nijubashi Bridge), which can also take you to Omotesando and Yoyogi Park.

Nezu no Ya

Address: 1-1-14 Nezu, Bunkyo-ku, Tokyo
How to get there: from Nezu Station, take Exit 1. Cross the street on your left, and then immediately turn left again into the little side street. Look for the entrance with lots of plants and wood. Walking distance from Ueno Park.

Opening hours: daily except Sundays, lunch from 11:30 to 15:30, café time between 15:30 and 17:00.
Price: 800~1200 yen for lunch, cake sets 800 yen.

A spritely old hand in Tokyo's vegan world, little Nezu no Ya has been around since 1978! Combining both a restaurant and an attached natural foods store, it feels like you have wandered into a grandmother's kitchen. The lunch sets and dessert choices are limited and made clear in the English menus, but whipped up with the skill of decades. The daily special is worth a gander as it changes constantly, while still hitting the spot every time. From giant veggie-stuffed spring rolls with a nicely contrasting marinated cabbage side one early summer day, to a braised tofu/mushroom dish on a chilly winter afternoon, these dishes makes the usual accompaniment of rice and miso soup shine. The typical Japanese version of a 'ploughman's lunch', two rice balls with miso soup and pickles, is perfect for light eaters. During lunch hours, desserts and drinks are discounted to just 200 yen each. Since portions can be a bit modest, this is a perfect excuse to round out your meal with something sweet.

Mejiro

Home to Gakushuin University, the alma mater of several members of the Imperial Family, this predominantly residential area is quiet and prosperous. While pretty unnoteworthy, the neighborhood boasts an attractive traditional Japanese garden called Mejiro Teien as well as the small Philatelic Museum, which may be of interest to stamp collectors. Nonetheless, it is well worth a visit to sample some of Tokyo's biggest, juiciest veggie burgers.

Mejiro is on the Yamanote Line, right between the much busier Ikebukuro and Takadanobaba districts, and only a couple stops away from central Shinjuku Station.

Vegetarian Beast

Address: 3-14-18 Mejiro, Toshima-ku, Tokyo
How to get there: from Mejiro Station's only exit, head towards the left and immediately cross the large street. Take the little road towards the right that follows the train tracks, and walk straight for a couple minutes. Look for the restaurant's black and white sign.
Opening hours: open Thursday to Sunday from 11:00 to 16:00.
Price: 1000~2000 yen, extra side dishes 500 yen

While the restaurant's name might seem a bit intimidating, it clearly broadcasts the owner's intention to provide soul-satisfying meals that can win over even inveterate carnivores. Mainly known for their bodacious burgers, you can customize your order to suit your tastes and appetite. Choose from single, double or even triple patties for your Beast Burger and finish it off with the sauce of your choice. The tangy BBQ and Original Spicy Sauce give a good kick of 'junky' delight, but the demi-glace sauce is also a winner. If you still have a bit of room, order a side of their excellent lasagna or pickled escabeche.

Komagome

Off towards the quieter section of the Yamanote Line, you will find two fine, contrasting examples of gardens nearby. Rikugien is a traditional Edo era strolling garden, which is particularly pretty in the fall. A 15-minute walk away is Kyu-Furukawa, which boasts an attractive Meiji era Western-style residence and a combination of Japanese and European-style gardens, including a colorful rose garden.

Komagome is on the Yamanote Line, just one stop away from Sugamo and it's famous "granny shopping street," and just a few stops away from major spots like

Ueno, Ikebukuro and Nippori. It is also on the Namboku Line, which can connect you to Todai-mae—home to Tokyo University's rather grand, attractive campus—and Korakuen, where you can find another one of Tokyo's elegant gardens, as well as a small amusement park.

Nourish

Address: 2F Ishikawa Kopo, 1-37-8 Komagome, Toshima-ku, Tokyo
How to get there: from the JR Line's South Exit take a left, passing the Hotel Mets. At the intersection take a right, after the next small crossing you should see the restaurant's orange sign.
Opening hours: open daily except on Wednesdays and New Year holidays, lunch from 11:30 to 14:30 (last order at 14:00) and dinner from 18:00 to 22:30 (last order at 21:30).
Price: 1000~1980 yen for lunch, around 3500 yen for dinner.

Homey, well-priced and truly delicious, Nourish should be high on the list of any vegan—including oriental vegans—who visits Tokyo. The lunch sets are a steal, as the 1980 yen Nourish Set includes your choice of main dish, salad, rice, miso soup, dessert and a drink.

Their most famous dish is a vegan rendition of 'chicken *nanban*', a delightful combination of fried soy meat covered in a sweet-savory sauce and topped with a giant dollop of homemade tartar sauce. Other satisfying standouts are the 'Asian plate' (a veganized version of Hainanese chicken rice) and glazed teriyaki cutlets on a bed of fresh salad. Each dish is bright, flavorful and distinct, down to the last bite of their rich chocolate brownies and chestnutty Mont Blanc. If visiting on a weekend go early, as they are understandable popular and tend to fill up quickly.

A Little Extra Gift: A Few Tips for Kyoto

While this is indeed a vegan guide to Tokyo, Kyoto is the second most visited city in Japan, and equally blessed with many vegan-friendly restaurants. I have visited the city many times and although this is only a small sampling of the restaurants available, just think of it as a starting point for your gourmet explorations.

Kyoto is a lovely but somewhat confusing city, very much divided between the hillside areas and the flats. Many of the most famous temples and shrines lie closer to the foot of the mountains, while the central grid is more modern, though still filled with wonderful discoveries in the side streets and covered markets. Everyone should make their own memories and adventures in the ancient capital, but one thing I would absolutely recommend is an early morning visit to Nanzenji Temple and its incongruous aqueduct, followed by a leisurely stroll down the Philosopher's Path all the way to Ginkakuji Temple, also known as the Golden Pavilion. Getting there early will allow you to miss the busloads of tourists, and work up a good appetite for a delicious lunch.

Let me share three of my favorite restaurants in Kyoto, and have a great time discovering more on your own during your stay in the city of one thousand temples.

Ukishima Garden

Address: 543 Asakura-cho, Nakagyo-ku, Kyoto
How to get there: a short walk from Nishiki Market. From Exit 9 of Kawaramachi Station face the large road and walk to the right, to the entrance of the Teramachi Dori shopping street. Walk down the shopping street and take the fourth left onto Rokkaku Dori street. Walk straight and take the 3rd right, a little after a small park. It is the fourth building on the right.

Opening hours: daily except Wednesdays, dinner between 17:00 to 22:00 (last order 21:00).
Price: dinner courses starting at 3800 yen, with a la carte around 1000 yen per dish.

An absolute gem in a city of fantastic restaurants, their contemporary version of *shojin ryori* (Buddhist cuisine) is both inventive and perfectly executed. The elegant Japanese garden, sleek wood counters and antique lamps create a haven in which to enjoy their entirely vegan menu. The millet and Kyoto vegetable gratin combines caramelized local seasonal veggies with a rich, browned covering, and the fried 'fish' and carrot 'prawns' are crisp and satisfying. The wafting smell of their *tantan* ramen alone may tempt you back for a second round. Many gluten free options are available, with English menus and well-spoken staff.

Veg Out

Address: 1F Kamogawa Bldg. 448 Inari-cho, Shimogyo-ku, Kyoto
How to get there: from Shichijo Station, take Exit 3 and walk across the bridge, the restaurant is in the first building on the other side.
Opening hours: daily except Mondays, from 08:00 to 21:00 (last order 20:00).
Price: lunch between 1000~1500 yen, budget 2000~3000 yen for dinner.

This airy café has a great view of the Kamogawa River and the nearby bridge, and is only a 15 minute walk from Kyoto Station, making it a convenient spot to stop on your first or last day in town. The *obanzai* plate, a Kyoto-style veggie-based version of tapas, is a good option for lunch as you can sample a variety of the old capital's cuisine in one go. The falafel are flavorful and perfectly cooked, crunchy on the outside with a smooth, moist texture. The vegan quiche is one of the best renditions around, stuffed with plenty of veggies to add texture. On the way out, buy a couple muffins to go, perfect for snacks or breakfast the following morning.

Morpho Cafe

Address: 309 Saikachi-cho, Kamigyo-ku, Kyoto
How to get there: from Nijojo Mae Station, exit the station and find the main entrance to Nijo Castle. Keeping the castle on your left, you will walk down the main road (Horikawa Dori). Keep on walking for about 15 minutes, crossing streets seven times. The restaurant is on the left, right after an old-fashioned shopping arcade.
Opening hours: daily except Tuesdays, lunch from 11:45 to 14:30 (last order at 14:00) and dinner from 17:00 to 20:30 (last order 20:00). May also be closed on other days, check their Twitter account to be sure.
Price: 850~1200 yen for lunch, a bit more for dinner. Giving them a call at 075-432-5017 before you go is recommended (English spoken).

Morpho may be a bit far from major stations and have slightly erratic hours, but the relaxing atmosphere and vegan comfort food which dances on the line between junk food and healthiness have brought it a steady fan base. The husband and wife team whip up a large selection of dishes ranging from Japanese vegan classics (deep fried *katsu* cutlets and ramen) to more Western-style favorites such as a bodacious veggie burger and soy cream pasta. The potato and corn cream pizza, a vegan reinvention of Japan's famously odd pizzas, is velvety and indulgent. Leave space for their daily sweets, and opt for the fruit tart if it is available.

Helpful Hints and Tips for Visitors

While having a list of restaurants is great, there are times when you want a quick snack or need to keep to a strict budget. Japan is a wonderfully convenient country, and the sheer variety of Tokyo's offerings means that there are several options for eating on the go or a cheap-and-cheerful impromptu picnic in your hotel or one of the city's many parks.

Please do note that because food companies do not always list every single ingredient, there is a chance that there could be a small amount of animal derivatives, amino acids or potentially even stock that is not listed on the package. While some vegans are okay with this, others are not, so if you are uncomfortable with this stick to non-processed foods like fruits and veggies.

Convenience Stores

Finding a *conbini* (convenience store) in Tokyo is rarely an issue, as sometimes it seems like there is one on every street corner. But the best option for vegan and gluten free friendly meals is Natural Lawson, a fancier and supposedly more health conscious version of the ubiquitous Lawson chain.

These stores always have a stock of vegan and gluten free bars, some of which indicate this on the packaging in English, as well as a selection of macrobiotic cookies made by Biokura. Along with fresh cut fruit, dried fruits, nuts and even a small selection of gluten free bread produced by Maisen, this is the easiest and most reliable spot to find something to munch on. The chilled section usually has a good stock of soy milk, sometimes in seasonal flavors, along with almond milk, pre-packaged fruit and veggie smoothies. There will often be individual packets of tofu and some of the *onigiri* rice balls are also safe and have a bit of English on the package. Make sure to check the cup noodle section to see if they have T's Tantan ramen, which is both vegan and delicious. The stock does change, so take some time to explore the racks and see what goodies are available. With over 120 stores located in important parts of the city, you are sure to run into one at least a few times during your time in Tokyo.

Other convenience stores such as Seven-Eleven, Family Mart, Sunkus and Circle K have varying degrees of English-language signage, so can be a bit of an adventure. A reliable standby in most cases will be the *konbu* (seaweed), *ume* (pickled plum), *sekihan* (a reddish mixture of rice and adzuki beans) or plain salt *onigiri*. *Inari sushi*, sweetened fried tofu pouches stuffed with rice, may look vegan however they are usually soaked in fish broth. Kikkoman-brand soy milk, recognizable by the brand name in English and the logo of a bird flying towards the sun, is commonly available and usually located by the juice boxes. Pickled veggies, single-serving sized tofu sets, salted *edamame* soy beans and simple packaged salads are also easy to find.

Supermarkets

Japanese supermarkets can be beguiling, but the almost complete lack of English and unhelpful packaging make them a bit intimidating.

Much like convenience stores, simple prepared foods such as cut fruit, salads and rice balls, as well as microwavable packs of rice, are quite common. In the deli section there will be a lot of animal-based foods, but things like salted *edamame*, pickles and noodles- without the sauce, which is sure to contain fish, are available in most stores. Tofu is abundant and absolutely delicious, even when just topped with a drizzle of soy sauce or salt. Keep your eye out for *goma dofu*, little packs of black sesame tofu often stocked in the same area as the regular version, which is wonderfully rich and quite hard to find outside of Japan.

In the dairy section you can find soy milk- the characters for soy milk are 豆乳. Do be careful of which color the package is: the green ones are processed (and so a bit smoother and sweeter), while the brown ones are unsweetened and taste quite strongly of beans. There is also a brand of soy yogurt, unfortunately only available in large containers, produced by Marusan. You may see smaller pots of soy yogurt produced by Soyafarm, but they contain gelatin so are best avoided.

While they look very tempting, breads in supermarkets should be skipped, as they are almost invariably not vegan.

Specialty Stores

Just as in any other large city, Tokyo has a big population of consumers who want safe, organic and health food, supplements and supplies. There are a couple of smaller grocers (such as the store attached to Nezu no Ya), and some larger suppliers.

The most common is Natural House, which is listed in the Harajuku/Omotesando section of this guide. While the main store has an eat-in space, most of the other branches are smaller. They certainly have a selection of vegan, gluten free and allergen free options varying from curries to desserts, but unfortunately much of the packaging is often only in Japanese, and the prices can be quite high. One more thing to keep in mind is that they often label their products as vegetarian when they are actually vegan. If you are unsure, just take the product you wish to buy to the staff and show them the vegan card included in this guide. They will be happy to double check for you.

There are 15 Natural House shops in central Tokyo, and the following are those located in popular sightseeing areas:

Yurakucho Itocia Branch

Address: 2-7-1 Yurakucho, Chiyoda-ku, Tokyo
Located in Ginza, the Itocia department store is right in front of the Central Exit of JR Yurakucho Station, or just a minute or two walk from the C9 Exit of Ginza Station. The shop is in the basement (B1).

Atre Kichijoji Branch

Address: 1-1-24 Kichijoji Minamicho, Musashino-shi, Tokyo

This shop is located in the Atre department store directly connected to Kichijoji Station, you will find it on the first floor of the main building.

Atre Meguro Branch

Address: 2-16-9 Kamiosaki, Shinagawa-ku, Tokyo
Located on the second floor of the Atre department store, which is connected to Meguro Station towards the East Exit.

Nihonbashi Takashimaya Branch

Address: 2-4-1 Nihonbashi, Chuo-ku, Tokyo
One of the smallest shops, hidden away on the B1 floor of the elegant Takashimaya department store. Directly connected to Exit B2 of Nihonbashi Station, or a short walk from Tokyo Station's Yaesu North Exit. Walking straight across a large road, passing a section of cheap eateries and office buildings, you should see the bright red logo as you come onto Chuo Street, right across from the large Maruzen bookstore.

Juices/Smoothies and Salads

For a quick breakfast or snack on the go, Tokyo has an increasing number of cold-pressed juice, smoothie and salad spots, usually located in more fashionable areas around the city. While many offerings are pretty similar to those you would find in juice or salad bars around the world, keep an eye out for matcha-flavored items, as the grade of tea used in Japan is usually higher and really gives a full, earthy kick to drinks. Pricewise expect to pay at least 800 yen and up for anything described below.

While there are several options around town, the following are a few essential favorites in convenient locations:

Parachutes (Shinjuku)

Address: 3-30-31 Shinjuku, Shinjuku-ku, Tokyo
Opening hours: weekdays from 09:00 to 21:00, weekends and holidays from 09:00 to 20:30.

Serves fresh cold pressed juices and one basic vegan sandwich. Located on the ground floor of the Marui department store, which is right by Exit A2 of Shinjuku Sanchome Station.

Cosme Kitchen JUICERY (Shibuya)

Address: 2-21-1 Shibuya, Shibuya-ku, Tokyo
Opening hours: weekdays from 08:00 to 21:00, weekends and holidays from 10:00 to 21:00.

Located on the second floor of the fancy Hikarie ShinQs department store, which connects directly with Shibuya Station, this little shop serves a few light snacks, cold pressed juices and smoothies to go.

Salad Stop! (Omotesando)

Address: 4-4-13 Jingumae, Shibuya-ku, Tokyo
Opening hours: daily from 11:00 to 21:00.

The first Japanese branch of a Singaporean salad bar chain. From Exit A2 of Omotesando Station go straight and take the first right after the Apple store. Take a left at the Flying Tiger shop and turn at the next right. It is in the fourth building on your right.

Sky High Raw Juice (Omotesando)

Address: Aoyama TN Bldg, 2-3-4 Shibuya, Shibuya-ku, Tokyo
Opening hours: Monday to Saturday from 10:00 to 19:00, Sundays 12:00 to 17:00.

Besides juices and smoothies, this little shop near Omotesando Station also has a small selection of vegan and raw salad bowls, smoothie bowls and vegan muffins. Just a couple doors down from 8ablish.

Crisp Salad Works (Roppongi)

Address: 6-10-1 Roppongi, Minato-ku, Tokyo
Opening hours: daily from 11:00 to 22:00.

Based on American made-to-order salad bars, this shop is located on the 1st floor of the Hillside section of the massive Roppongi Hills complex. All the dressings are gluten free, and the menu clearly indicates which ingredients are vegan or gluten free.

Sweets and Treats

While it is often said that most Japanese desserts are vegan by default, this is not necessarily true. While some make their *mochi* (rice cake) sweets fresh every day, more broadly commercially available rice sweets often contain some egg white to help keep the rice soft. And even so, every once in a while the craving for a sweeter, more elaborate treat just needs to be satisfied.

Since 2017 there has been a small boom of shops offering vegan ice cream sundaes and donuts, much to the glee of many vegans in search of a real sugar fix! As they are considered rather trendy it is best to visit early on in the day to avoid disappointment or long lines.

Doughnut Plant Yurakucho

Address: Tokyo International Forum, Hall C 1F, 3-5-1 Marunouchi, Chiyoda-ku, Tokyo
How to get there: Located near Yurakucho Station or Tokyo Station, follow the signs for Tokyo International Forum. The shop is small and located towards the back of Hall C.
Opening hours: weekdays 08:00 to 19:00, weekends and holidays from 09:00 to 19:00.
Price: around 350 yen for a donut.

Unlike the original New York branch, the Tokyo store usually has two seasonal vegan options made with a soy milk base, which can range from matcha frosted rings to delightful coconut-based confections. Interestingly, even their non-vegan donuts do not contain eggs, making them safe for those with egg allergies. To avoid disappointment, I recommend checking this spot between 09:00 to 16:00, as they do tend to sell out and the donuts are best when they are fresh.

Good Town Doughnuts

Address: 6-12-6 Jingumae, Shibuya-ku, Tokyo
How to get there: take Exit 4 from Meiji Jingumae Station, and walk straight ahead crossing the major road. Turn right, and walk straight until the second tiny side street to the left, right before the Arc'teryx store. Walk straight down, then take a right at the post office. Keep on going, you will soon see the shop on your right.
Opening hours: daily, 10:00 to 20:00.
Price: 380~420 yen yen for a donut, 600 yen for the almond milk latte.

Just off of trendy Cat Street, this little joint is valhalla for donut lovers. Every day they make a handful of vegan versions of their sweet treats, which are kept in a separate case next to the non-vegan varieties. It is best to go early in the day because they do sell out, and you don't want to miss the perfectly moist dough, covered with decadent glazes that manage to be diabetes-inducing but vibrant at the same time. The sicilian lemon-poppy donut's glaze is fresh and intense, and their signature smiley mango ones are sure to put a smile on your face too. If you want to add a caffeine rush to your sugar high, they offer almond milk lattes and American-style coffee with free refills.

Kippy's Coco-Cream

Address: Sendagaya RF Bldg, 2-6-3 Sendagaya, Shibuya-ku, Tokyo
How to get there: about a 10 minute walk from Harajuku Station. After coming out of the Main Exit for JR Harajuku Station, take a right and follow the large road until you get to the Nespresso Café. Turn right and just keep on going straight. The shop is just past the Sendagaya Elementary School.
Opening hours: daily from 11:00 to 19:30.
Price: 600~700 yen for a couple of scoops, a little more if you select toppings.

A California import, the creamy coconut-based desserts are worth the walk. All the flavors are made with as few ingredients as possible and no processed sugar, so no flighty sugar highs here! The thickness of the coconut cream is very close to dairy-based ice cream, and doesn't get the odd icy texture common with soy or rice milk. The cinnamon and coffee date double scoop is a favorite, and the seasonal specials are always something to look forward to. One disclaimer: most of the flavors include raw honey, however there are always a few that use dates to sweeten the coconut cream instead. It is all written out clearly, so no worries about accidentally getting a honey-based one. They share space with a juice and shake shop, in case you want to sneak in some (rather pricey) fruits and veggies.

Wanokashi

Address: 3-2-1 Uehara, Shibuya-ku, Tokyo
How to get there: from Yoyogi-Uehara Station, take either of the South Exits and go right. Keep walking straight until the road ends, and take a left. You should see the broad Inokashira Dori street in front of you. Cross the street and go left, following the large road. Walk for about 5 minutes, until the first street on your right (look for the green street lamps). Turn right into this smaller street, and go straight. Right after passing a small side street on your right, you should be able to see the sweets shop, recognizable by a small blue flag with a white circle flying from a pointy white building.
Opening hours: open daily except Mondays between 10:30 to 18:00.
Price: around 300~400 yen for each sweet.

For fans of *wagashi* (Japanese sweets) or those curious to try them for the first time, Wanokashi is a 100% vegan haven. Most of them are also gluten free, with the exception of sweets that use soy sauce containing traces of wheat. They are most famous for their *fukumeguri daifuku*, soft rice cakes filled with agave-sweetened red and black bean paste. However they also have puddings, cookies and the delightful *emikoboreruan*, literally 'smile-inducing sweets' that combine chocolate with matcha bean paste, pumpkin paste or other seasonal flavors.

Wired Bonbon

Address: Lumine Shinjuku 1 6F, 1-1-5 Nishishinjuku, Shinjuku-ku, Tokyo
How to get there: the café is housed inside the Lumine 1 department store, which connects almost directly with Shinjuku Station's South Exit.
Opening hours: daily from 11:00 to 22:30 (last order at 21:45).
Price: from 730~1280 yen, depending on the elaborateness of the dessert.

Wired is a good description of what one feels like after a visit to this temple dedicated to towering ice cream parfaits and fluffy french toast. The clearly marked menus overflow with delights such as colorful soy milk-based ice cream sundaes, cruelty free green tea tiramisu, berry-stuffed crepes and other vegan seasonal specials, so sugar fiends will truly be spoiled for choice. If visiting on a weekend make sure to go early in the day, as the vegan ice cream tends to sell out quickly.

Coffee Chains

Tokyo runs on coffee, so you will find plenty of coffee and tea chains around the city. As usual Starbucks is very good at serving the vegan community, as most drinks can be switched to soy or almond milk for a small additional charge of 50 yen. Staff members are also usually careful to ask about whipped cream and other additions, making it a stress-free experience. While the coffee is pretty much the same all over the world, the Matcha Latte (green tea latte) is made using much higher-quality tea, so is a must-try as an alternative to your morning cup of Arabica. Another only-in-Japan item is the rather addictive Hojicha Latte, made with roasted green tea which gives off a deep, slightly smoky aroma.

The Seattle-based chain Tully's and local Doutor coffee shops also have soy milk-based coffee and tea drinks, but be careful about more fanciful options, as there may be some condensed milk or honey lurking in your cup.

Chain Restaurants

Most of the chains in Tokyo will be unfamiliar to visitors, but this is of little importance as almost all of them are not good options for those with plant-based diets. Fortunately in the run-up to the 2020 Olympics there is an increasing interest in catering to visitors and their dietary needs, so it's now possible to find a few choices.

CURRY HOUSE CoCo Ichibanya

This huge curry chain can be found near almost any large-ish train station, and purveys plates of Japanese-style curry and rice for around 500 to 700 yen. It is easily recognizable by the yellow and brown sign, which also shows a bowl of curry. While most of their curries contain meat of some description, including those labelled as vegetable curries, they have two options for visitors with special diets.

At 172 of their branches around Japan, including many in Tokyo, they offer a 'Vegetarian Curry' which is 100% vegan. The full list of shops offering this curry is available on their site, unfortunately in Japanese only. In addition, at all branches there is also an 'Allergen-Free Curry', which is sealed in a separate pouch. The only catch is that it contains traces of honey, which the majority of vegans avoid, but it is definitely gluten free, halal and even peanut free!

While not the most exciting meal, you can add some interest by selecting a few additional vegetable toppings such as spinach, tomato and asparagus, eggplant or even the infamous *natto* (fermented soybeans) if you are feeling adventurous. There are a couple of simple salads, which can also be spiced up with toppings like corn, okra and yam or pickled scallions, although you will want to stick to the oil-free dressing to avoid dairy or fish byproducts. The menu is available in English, Chinese, Korean, Thai, Russian, Arabic, Spanish and Portuguese, making ordering very simple.

Ootoya

Another chain that can be found around most busy stations, Ootoya is known for its well-priced and healthy home-style Japanese food. Look for a dark blue sign with white characters, and OOTOYA written out in English underneath.

While most of the menu does include animal products of some sort, they do have a few dishes that are vegan. Their homemade tofu is good, just ask for it without *katsuobushi* bonito flakes, and the sesame-dressed spinach is another safe option. The fried vegetables in a black vinegar sauce are also vegan-friendly, and along with a bowl of regular white rice or '5 grain rice' you can create a decent, healthy meal that doesn't break your budget. While none of the desserts are vegan, the 'black sugar soy milk' drink is pretty tasty, although may be overly sweet for some. Ootoya waiters are often non-Japanese and can speak a bit of English, and English menus are available at most branches.

Mr. FARMER

Part of the successful Eatwalk restaurant group, there are four branches of the farm-to-table Mr. FARMER around Tokyo. As the menu is based around West Coast health food favorites, the vegan options tend to lean towards veggie burgers, burritos and salads. The desserts are usually always vegan and often include a gluten free option, with fresh 'cheesecakes' and berry tiramisu available at most branches. The burdock burger is flavored with curry and topped with creamy mayonnaise, which gives it a decent heft. While staff may not speak English, the menus make it clear which items are vegan, gluten free and even low carb! Do keep in mind that the prices are on par with the trendiness of the restaurants. Expect around 1600 to 2000 yen for a basic lunch, with desserts around 750 yen, and note that tax is not included on the menu prices. Weekends are very busy, so best avoided unless you are prepared to wait.

Omotesando Branch

Address: Sepia Harajuku 1F, 4-5-12 Jingumae, Shibuya-ku, Tokyo
Opening hours: daily from 09:00 to 20:00.

From Exit A2 of Omotesando Station go straight and take the first right after the Apple store. Take a left at Flying Tiger and then your next right. It is a couple buildings down from Salad Stop! on the right side.

Shinjuku Mylord Branch

Address: Mosaic Street, 1-1-3 Nishishinjuku, Shinjuku-ku, Tokyo
Opening hours: daily from 09:00 to 23:00.

This branch is located in an area called Mosaic Street, right between Shinjuku Station and the oddly named Mylord department store. It is possible to get there from both the East Exit and South Exit of Shinjuku Station, but it can be a bit confusing. They stay open until 23:00, very convenient for those looking for a bite to eat later in the evening.

Roppongi Branch

Address: 6-10-1 Roppongi, Minato-ku, Tokyo
Opening hours: daily from 11:00 to 23:00.

Easy to find, this branch is housed on level B2 of Roppongi Hills' Hillside section, and is also open until 23:00.

Komazawa Olympic Park Branch

Address: 1-1-2 Komazawakoen, Setagaya-ku, Tokyo
Opening hours: daily from 07:00 to 21:00.

From Komazawa Daigaku Station you will take the Komazawa Park Exit, going up the stairs to your right. From there walk straight ahead for about 10 minutes, until you get to a large four-way intersection. On the opposite side of the street you should see a huge vertical sign with black characters and a red arrow pointing to the left. Turn left, without crossing the street, and go straight for about 5 minutes. You should soon see a low wall decorated with odd paintings. Follow it until it ends, the restaurant will be on your left in the entrance of the park.

A bit further out than the others, this is probably the prettiest and most café-like of all the Mr.FARMER branches.

Nataraj

This small chain of restaurants specializes in organic veggie-based Indian cuisine, and offers both vegetarian and vegan-friendly dishes, including 100% vegan naan. As they are open until 23:00 (with last order at 22:30), Nataraj can help you out in extremis. The restaurants are in convenient and commonly visited locations:

Ginza Branch

Address: Ginza Kosaka Bldg 7-9F, 6-9-4 Ginza, Chuo-ku, Tokyo
Opening hours: daily from 11:30 to 23:00 (last order at 22:30), closed during New Years.

Take Exit A2 of Ginza Station and walk straight. Cross the first street that you come to, and the restaurant is in the 2nd building on your right.

Shibuya Milan Nataraj Branch

Address: Iwamoto Bldg 3F, 1-22-7 Jinnan, Shibuya-ku, Tokyo

Opening hours: daily from 11:30 to 23:00 (last order at 22:30), closed during New Years.

From Exit 7a of Shibuya Station, take an immediate right onto Inokashira Dori road. You will pass the 109 Men's department store on your right. Keep on going straight until you pass the Marui department store. The restaurant is on the 3rd floor of the skinny, dark glass-fronted building right after it.

Minami Aoyama Branch

Address: Miwa Aoyama Bldg B1F, 2-22-19 Minamiaoyama, Minato-ku, Tokyo
Opening hours: daily from 11:30 to 23:00 (last order at 22:30), closed during New Years

From Gaienmae Station, go straight out of Exit 1b. You will see a pedestrian overpass ahead of you, walk towards it. Right after the overpass, look for a small green awning on your right. The restaurant is not far from the famous Gaienmae Ginko Tree Avenue.

Ogikubo Branch

Address: Fukumura Sangyou Bldg B1, 5-30-6 Ogikubo, Suginami-ku, Tokyo
Opening hours: daily from 11:30 to 23:00 (last order at 22:30), closed during New Years.

From Ogikubo Station's South B Exit, take an immediate right into the small shopping street, then take the first left you come to. The restaurant is in the 4th building on your left.

Farmer's Markets and Festivals

Tokyo hosts several vegan and health food oriented festivals each year, as well as two outdoor markets in the Omotesando/Aoyama area where one can find vegan and natural goodies on a more regular basis.

COMMUNE

Address: 3-13 Minami-Aoyama, Minato, Tokyo
How to get there: from Exit A4 of Omotesando Station go right, and then take another right when you reach the large road (Aoyama Dori). Walk for a couple minutes, and you will see the sign and stalls on your right.
Open daily

This fun combination of outdoor market/event space is open every day, with a variety of interesting stalls to explore and people to meet. Check out Cori. Vegan Foodstand, which is open between 13:00 to 21:00 every day except Mondays, for solid basics like falafel, salads and other goodies. Make sure to cruise around the pop-up stands too, as there may be some cool crafts, foods or fashion available.

Farmer's Market @UNU

Address: in front of the United Nations University, 5-53-70 Jingumae, Shibuya-ku, Tokyo
How to get there: about a 5 minute walk from Exit B2 of Omotesando Station, walk straight until you reach an intersection. Cross and keep on going straight. You will cross two smaller crosswalks, until you see the step-like UN University building and the white tents of the market.
Open on weekends between 10:00 to 16:00

Tokyo's most famous farmer's market, if you want organic veggies, hand-pressed juices, artisan bread or pretty crafts, be sure to stop by on Saturday or Sunday. While the stalls change weekly, you are almost certain to find at least a couple purveyors of vegan baked goods and some food trucks with plant-based dishes. Keep an eye out for Terra Burgers in particular.

Tokyo Vegefood Festa

When: usually held in October or November, exact dates change yearly
Where: Yoyogi Park Events Square

One of the biggest events on a Tokyo vegan's social calendar, this event brings in hundreds of stalls dedicated to all things vegetarian, vegan and natural. Lots of famous restaurants and food trucks put out stalls, and you could spend hours sampling all the yummy treats available. To beat the rush go a bit early (around 10:00 or 11:00 am), if not expect lines at all the most popular spots.

Earth Day Tokyo

When: April 22 to 23
Where: Yoyogi Park Events Square

Many of the stalls are run by NPOs, farmers and crafters, but there are plenty of vegan options to choose from. However be warned, there are also some organic meat sellers and animal-based food trucks in the mix.

Vegan Gourmet Festival

When: usually held on a Sunday in early October and late April, exact dates change yearly

Where: Kiba Park

While this event is quite excellent, attracting vegan stalls from all across the country to the beautiful Kiba Park, they rarely publish information in English. Information is available in Japanese on their website, and you can use the Google Chrome browser to help translate the page.

Useful Phrases and Japanese Words

All the businesses in this guide are vegan-friendly, and have a decent understanding of dietary restrictions. However non-vegan specific restaurants and shops may require a little more effort. While many eateries in Tokyo have been trying to improve the level of English they offer, either using menus or hiring employees with language skills, it is still helpful to have a bit of backup just in case.

In case you need to explain veganism to someone, show them the following phrase. Take a screenshot just in case, so you always have it on hand:

I am vegan, and do not eat meat, fish, seafood (including soup bases or flavorings) or any animal products (eggs, milk products, honey).
私はビーガンです。肉類、魚類、魚介類エキスと出汁含めて、また動物性の食品卵類、乳製品、ハチミツなどを食べられません。

If you want to ask if a dish contains animal products or allergens:

Does this contain ...?
...は入っていますか
...wa haitte imasuka?

English	Japanese	Pronunciation
Meat	肉	niku
Fish	魚	sakana
Shellfish	魚介	gyokai
Milk products	乳製品	nyuuseihin
Eggs	卵	tamago
Egg white	卵白	ranpaku
Honey	ハチミツ	hachimitsu
Beef	牛肉	gyuuniku
Pork	豚肉	butaniku
Chicken	鶏肉	toriniku
Animal-based extracts	動物性エキス	doubutsusei ekisu
Fish flakes	かつお節	katsuobushi
Wheat	小麦	komugi
Gluten	でん粉	denpun
Alcohol	アルコール	arukooru

If shopping or asking for substitutions, the following may prove helpful:

Excuse me, do you have...?
すみません、...ありますか
Sumimasen, ... arimasu ka?

If you wish to ask to have a particular ingredient removed or left out, then use the following phrase. You can insert the words mentioned in the section above, or more specific terms.

Be aware that snippets of cheese, ham, bacon and fish flakes tend to get sprinkled over a lot of dishes, so it is always good to check with the staff before ordering. Terms like cheese, bacon and ham are also used in Japanese, just make sure to speak slowly for non-English speakers.

Without ... please.
...抜きお願いします。
...nuki onegaishimasu.

As always when traveling around a foreign country, make sure to be upbeat and polite when asking staff for alterations. Causing a scene or being aggressive in Japan is definitely frowned upon, and a smile and multiple thank-yous are much more likely to get you what you want.

Last Thoughts and Remarks

I truly hope that this guide helps you enjoy the culinary delights of my beloved Tokyo and that you leave with great memories, a few cherished photos and an appreciation for vegan Japanese cuisine. I would love to hear from you, either at @tokyoveganguide or the #tokyoveganguide tag on Instagram or at veganguide.writer@gmail.com.

Did you find that a restaurant has closed or changed their menu completely? If so I apologize in advance. The day this book went live all the restaurants, shops and other services mentioned were open and in business. If you discover some change in operations, please let me know, and I will update the next version of the guide as well as announce it to the world at large in any way I can.

I wish to thank Tatsuro for patiently listening to me be snarky at my laptop and eating more than his fair share of brown rice. Much gratitude to Becky, Sarah, Anna, Nami, Mari and Deborah for joining me on the many restaurant outings required to compile the guide and their support for this project. More thanks go to my parents, who also inspired me to include information for those with gluten free and halal diets. The careful editing and advice of Lauren Shannon was invaluable, as were the photographic skills of Miho Fujioka and cover design chops of Nanako Honda.

And finally, thank you for purchasing my book and for choosing to live a little bit lighter and with more compassion towards our fellow creatures.

About the Author

Chiara Terzuolo began traipsing about Japan around 2007, and has been a Tokyo resident since 2011. A travel specialist and writer, she has written for various media, including Japan Today, GaijinPot, Savvy, Jetsetter and All About, as well as being featured on the Wall Street Journal and NHK.

Chiara spends a good deal of time exploring remote areas of Japan, looking for vegan-friendly local foods, coffee and a place to plug in her laptop. She was inspired to write her first book, the *Tokyo Vegan Guide*, to help the growing number of vegan visitors to Japan's capital find meals worthy of traveling across the ocean for. For updates on her never-ending quest for great vegan food, you can follow her on Instagram at @tokyoveganguide.

Tokyo Vegan Guide 2018

Table of Contents

Foreword	2
How to Use the Guide	3
Criteria for Choosing the Restaurants	4
Wait, What About...?	5
Popular Sightseeing Spots	6
Shinjuku	7
Kiboko	8
Ain Soph Ripple	8
Chaya Macrobiotics Isetan	9
Other Options in the Shinjuku Area	10
Futaba Fruits Parlor	10
Ain Soph Journey	11
Shibuya	11
Yaffa Organic Cafe	12
Nagi Shokudo	13
Tokyo Station Area	14
T's TanTan	15
Sora no Iro NIPPON	15
Ginza	16
Chaya Natural & Wild Table	17
Kyushu Jangara Ramen	18
Harajuku/Omotesando	19
8ablish	19
Hanada Rosso	20
Brown Rice Canteen	21
Tamana Shokudo	22
Other Options in the Harajuku/Omotesando Area	23
Sincere Garden	23
Mominoki House	23
Natural House Aoyama Branch	24
Trueberry	25
Asakusa Area	25
Kaemon Asakusa	26

Sasaya Cafe	27
Fucha Bon	28
Ueno	29
T's TanTan Ecute Ueno	30
Roppongi	30
Veganic to Go	31
Chien Fu	31
Other Options in Roppongi	32
AFURI	32
.RAW	33
Shimokitazawa	33
Chabuzen	34
Yoyogi Area	35
Tudore Tranquility	35
Other Options in the Yoyogi Area	36
Bojun Tomigaya	36
Ikebukuro	37
Senjyo Teuchi Gyoza Senmonten	38
Other Options in Ikebukuro	38
Ain Soph Soar	38
Off the Beaten Track	39
Hiroo	40
Trueberry	40
Vegan Cafe	41
Jimbocho	41
Loving Hut	42
Okubo	43
Saishokukenbi	44
Ebisu	44
KO-SO CAFE	45
Rainbow Raw Food/ Hemp Café	46
SUMI-BIO	47
Other Options in Ebisu	48
AFURI	48
Cosme Kitchen Adaptation	48

Dear My Body	49
Daikanyama	50
Blu Jam Cafe	50
Other Options in Daikanyama	51
Crisp Salad Works	51
Jiyugaoka	51
T's Restaurant	52
Shiro	53
Nakameguro	54
Rainbow Bird Rendevous	54
AFURI	55
Ogikubo and Nishi Ogikubo Area	56
Komenoko	56
Trim	57
Cafe Bask	58
Koenji Area	59
vege&grain cafe meu nota	59
Kitchen Cocomo	60
Kichijoji	61
Monk's Foods	62
Yanaka/Nezu/Sendagi	62
Nezu no Ya	63
Mejiro	64
Vegetarian Beast	65
Komagome	65
Nourish	66
A Little Extra Gift: A Few Tips for Kyoto	67
Ukishima Garden	67
Veg Out	68
Morpho Cafe	69
Helpful Hints and Tips for Visitors	69
Convenience Stores	70
Supermarkets	71
Specialty Stores	71
Yurakucho Itocia Branch	72
Atre Kichijoji Branch	72

Atre Meguro Branch	73
Nihonbashi Takashimaya Branch	73

Juices/Smoothies and Salads — 73
  Parachutes (Shinjuku) — 74
  Cosme Kitchen JUICERY (Shibuya) — 74
  Salad Stop! (Omotesando) — 74
  Sky High Raw Juice (Omotesando) — 75
  Crisp Salad Works (Roppongi) — 75

Sweets and Treats — 75
  Doughnut Plant Yurakucho — 76
  Good Town Doughnuts — 76
  Kippy's Coco-Cream — 77
  Wanokashi — 78
  Wired Bonbon — 78

Coffee Chains — 79

Chain Restaurants — 79
  CURRY HOUSE CoCo Ichibanya — 80
  Ootoya — 80
  Mr. FARMER — 81
    Omotesando Branch — 81
    Shinjuku Mylord Branch — 82
    Roppongi Branch — 82
    Komazawa Olympic Park Branch — 82
  Nataraj — 83
    Ginza Branch — 83
    Shibuya Milan Nataraj Branch — 83
    Minami Aoyama Branch — 84
    Ogikubo Branch — 84

Farmer's Markets and Festivals — 84
  COMMUNE — 85
  Farmer's Market @UNU — 85
  Tokyo Vegefood Festa — 86
  Earth Day Tokyo — 86
  Vegan Gourmet Festival — 86

Useful Phrases and Japanese Words — 87

Last Thoughts and Remarks — 90
About the Author — 90

95

Copyright © 2018 by Chiara Park Terzuolo

All rights reserved. This book or any portion thereof may not be reproduced or used in any manner whatsoever without the express written permission of the publisher except for the use of brief quotations in a book review.

ISBN: 978-1-64008-076-8

Although the author and publisher have made every effort to ensure that the information in this book was correct at press time, the author and publisher do not assume and hereby disclaim any liability to any party for any loss, damage, or disruption caused by errors or omissions, whether such errors or omissions result from negligence, accident, or any other cause. Furthermore, neither the author nor publisher has received any compensation, free goods or any other services from the businesses appearing in this book. The choice of businesses to include and opinions about their services lies exclusively with the author.

Printed in Great Britain
by Amazon